A MURDER REVISITED MYSTERY NOVEL: NO. 5

Dead and Not Buried

MURDER REVISITED SERIES

H. F. M. PRESCOTT

Dead and Not Buried

NEW YORK   THE MACMILLAN COMPANY   1954

CONTENTS

THE AUTHOR WISHES TO THANK MR. LAURENCE HOUSMAN FOR KIND PERMISSION TO QUOTE THE STANZAS FROM "A SHROPSHIRE LAD" APPEARING IN THE COURSE OF CHAPTER XV, AND ALL THOSE, IN CHARLBURY AND ELSEWHERE, WHO HAVE HELPED HER WITH INFORMATION, CRITICISM, OR ADVICE

1

EXIT MARSHALL

"LOCK THAT DOOR!"

The woman turned in the dark little passage, and leaned against the door, glad of the support it gave. She took a long time to turn the key in the lock because her fingers were shaking.

"Come on!" the man shouted. He too felt his knees quake, and the sound of his own voice was strange to him, but his instinct was to be doing something, and he had already gone through the farm kitchen and into the scullery beyond. "Come on! We've got to get this blood off our hands first." The creaking complaint of the pump and the gush and splash of water followed.

But the woman only got as far as the big chair by the fireplace, with its frilled cushion of faded cretonne.

"Come on!" the man shouted again, with a high note of frightened anger in his voice. "Get on with it. There's no time for hysterics. Get your hands washed or it will be all over your dress."

He came out of the scullery now, wiping his hands. His eyes were on her as she sat crouching there, her face changed, distorted, almost, as it were, unmade by shock and fear. She was not a pretty sight: he took his eyes away, and looked down at the towel he was using. It was a dank, dirty thing, and he vented on it the disgust he felt at the woman.

"Pah!" He threw it down on the floor. "Is that filthy rag your idea of a towel? It would be!" He pulled out a handkerchief, large, fine and fresh, and finished drying his hands on that.

The woman had not moved. With an exclamation he went over to her, and shook her, not too gently, by the shoulder.

"Get up! Don't you realize it's murder? Go and wash your hands." He was inclined to shout, but he remembered in time that they must keep quiet. They couldn't do with any passer-by talking about strange noises at Marshall's farm that afternoon.

She got up somehow and trailed out to the scullery door. But there she stood still.

"Oh! Oh! Take it away!"

He laughed. Her panic made him feel braver. "The gun? No, you've got to wash it first. I don't know where you keep your brushes and buckets and things. And the butt may have to stand in water for a bit to get it all off."

Her voice came again in a sort of shaking whisper, "There's —bits of hair on it."

"Damn you!" He felt very sick suddenly, and the kitchen was hot, airless, and strong smelling, as if the atmosphere was something more solid than ordinary air. He went over to the little window, and dragged apart the soiled lace curtains. On the sill a couple of drooping, dusty plants, an untidy heap of letters, bills, and advertisements, shared the space with spiders' webs. He put his hand on the iron catch and half pushed the window open on the dreary afternoon. But he slammed it again at once and fastened it.

"Damn!" he said. "Daren't have it open." He began to bite his nails. This was horrible, horrible. For a second he thought that it was so horrible that it could not be true. But it was true. An hour ago, half an hour ago, it would have seemed impossible. But now it was true.

Just then the woman came back into the kitchen. She had been crying, and now rubbed the back of her hand over her eyes. It was a clumsy gesture, and she ended it under her nose; then she snuffled.

The man looked at her with a fury of disgust. What comeliness she had—and not many would have seen comeliness in her strangely colourless face—was clean wiped out. "God!" he thought, "to think that I've got into this mess for a thing like that!"

She felt his eyes on her, and realized suddenly something of his feeling. Even now, when nothing really mattered but the thing that they had left behind them in the stable, she could not bear him to look at her so. Hastily she tried to straighten her hair; she managed to force a grotesque parody of the expression which, at the cinema, she had heard called "a woman's love look."

Ill-timed though her effort was, the man did not miss the significance of it. He laughed in her face.

"Trying to look like your portrait, are you?"

It was a relief to both of them to think, or at least to pretend to be thinking of something which belonged to the time before the last half hour—the half hour which had cut them off from all the ordinary safe past. The woman whipped herself into a shrill indignation.

"No I'm not. And I couldn't if I tried. It wasn't one bit like me, every one said it wasn't. And it squinted. And there were patches of blue on the face." She laughed hysterically. "Blue cheeks! I've not——"

"It got your 'come hither' look pretty well, anyway," he interrupted. "It was rather clever, *I* think; a good bit of work. But I suppose one can't expect you to be a judge of art."

He turned from her. "If it hadn't been for that damn' picture," he said savagely to the bland, blank face of the grandfather clock, "I'd never have come here."

He was startled by her voice when she blazed out at him; as it happened he had never heard women in a street row, and the ugliness of it made him recoil.

"Well and you can go," she screamed, "you—gentleman. Go on, get out of this!" Her voice ran up as she yelled abuse and foul names at him.

He listened for a moment, too startled to interrupt, then he put his hands on her shoulders and shook her till she staggered.

"Be quiet, will you! Do you want someone to hear you shouting and come in to see what it's about?"

That stopped her. He felt her cringe. She jerked her head towards the window, and stood silent, listening. Then she tried to wrench herself free.

"You did it," she cried, but not loudly now. "It wasn't me. It's none of my business." She repeated that, because she wanted to believe it.

He did not let her go, but shook her again, though more gently.

"Be quiet. Don't talk such rot. You're what they call an accessory after the fact; you just get that into your head." He looked at her a moment, calculating. "It's as bad, practically, as being"—he boggled at the word in his mind—"as the thing itself."

She muttered, "It's not. I didn't do anything." But he saw that she believed him.

"And they hang women in England. Don't you forget that." He drove the point home.

She began to cry, noisily and unrestrainedly, and in a huddle of words, all mixed up with gulps and sobs, to reproach him for what he had done. "What for did you want to hit him at all?" she cried at him. "You'd got the gun out of his hands. But you went on hitting and hitting him. Ugh!" She stopped. even fear of the future shut out for the moment by that picture in her mind—the old man down on the ground struggling to get up, and then one blow after another till—— She put her clenched fists up to her eyes.

The man saw it too. And he remembered how when he was hardly more than a child, he had seen a snake, the first he had ever seen. It had been a harmless grass snake, but he had not thought of that, and had chased it down the lane, hitting and hitting, in a panic of fear that was only increased by the sick disgust he felt as he saw the creature broken and dying. And that was how he had felt again this afternoon at the sight of old Marshall, horribly battered yet still faintly struggling. He could not stop hitting till the thing at his feet did not move any more.

But he was not going to confess that panic to any one; least of all to the woman. He cast about for some answer, and could find none but a sneer. "Devoted wife!" he said, and managed to laugh somehow.

She was still snivelling, but she stopped so suddenly that he looked at her, startled. She had her head turned stiffly over her shoulder. She was listening.

"Hush!" she whispered, though there was no need, for he stood silent and rigid, listening too.

"That was the stable door. Someone's gone in."

He felt his throat jerk. They waited.

From the yard outside came again the sound of a heavy door clapping against its latch. They waited still, for a footstep, for a shout.

The sound came again. The man gave a gasp and a sort of angry laugh.

"It can't be that door. I know I fastened it. It must be some other, and it's the wind that's swinging it."

"There isn't any wind," she objected.

"It can't be anything else," he snapped at her. "Joe's gone to market. You said yourself he won't be back tonight." He listened for a moment longer, then, giving his shoulders a shake, moved over to the table and sat down in the shabby armchair that had used to engulf, every evening, and every Sunday afternoon, the small, lean, stringy person of Farmer Marshall. Now his murderer sat there, and the farmer was only a highly inconvenient, and very unpleasant looking body, which had to be disposed of somehow.

The woman broke in. She was not content to see him sitting there, frowning, and drumming with his fingers on the arm of the chair.

"What are you going to do? We've got to do something quick. We can't leave him in the stable there. Any one might go in."

Her turned on her.

"Be quiet! I've got to think. It's no use being in a hurry." It was hard enough to get a hold over his own courage, let alone to think, and her fears made it harder yet. "Be quiet!" he almost shouted at her.

After a few moments he spoke again, but half to himself. "It's a good thing we've kept it so dark that no one knows we've been—fooling about together."

"Someone does—did," she said.

"Who? Marshall?"

She nodded. "That was why he stayed back today. To catch us, the old devil."

As she spoke she was staring at the chimney shelf, as though something there explained her words.

"What is it?" The man followed the direction of her eyes. When she did not answer, he got up and went to see for himself.

"Oh!" he said, and again "Oh!" and stood a long time looking into the fire. Once he smiled, but the smile was too like a dog's grin to be pleasant. When at last he turned round the woman stopped twitching at her clothes and fumbling with her hair. His face startled her; she had never seen him look like that before.

"This is what we'll do," he said, and told her. He even laughed while he told her. He thought it was very clever.

2

YORKE TAPS ON A WINDOW

IT WAS DARK, and a dripping thick dark—when Marc Yorke—his parents had spelt his name Mark—drove the car into the garage at Miller's Green. The garage was really an old stable and still kept its mangers and its ladder to the hay loft. As it was more roomy than was necessary for Yorke's Riley, the car shared it with a jumble of less elegant and highly polished articles, such as the gardening tools, some coils of rope, and an old bicycle. The collection of oddments sometimes encroached upon the space so much that Yorke, who though a young man had already a passion for neatness, would take off his expensive fur-lined driving gloves, and re-arrange the sliding moraine of nondescript articles, stacking them up into some sort of stability.

So now, when he had switched off the engine, and muffled the bonnet in an old travelling rug, he stood for a minute, re-viewing, with some distaste it seemed, the disorder of the old stable, partially illuminated by the raking glare of the head-lights. From the front of the car he moved along to the twi-light space beyond the radius of the lamps, and gathered up a handful of old sacks off the untidy heap. There were five. He folded each separately and neatly. Four were old, good only for covering cold frames, but one was whole, strong and

13

new. He laid it on top of the pile, then drew out one of the old ones and put that on top. Satisfied with the arrangement he looked about for a place to lay the bundle. The manger was full of pea sticks; he reached up and hung the sacks over one of the upper rungs of the stable ladder; they would be out of the way there, but handy when wanted. He switched off the head lamps, collected from the back seat an armful of parcels and a few library books, switched off the roof light, and stood for a second till his eyes could see in the faint twilight.

The old farm house of Miller's Green was a long low building across whose late eighteenth century front a nineteenth century owner had built one of those graceful, slightly fantastic, frivolous, and Brightonish iron verandas, a thing very pretty in sunshine, but now, on this dismal February evening, a dim gawky skeleton very inadequately draped with rails of wet and withered honeysuckle. The path from the garage ran right across the front of the house, and as Yorke came round the corner a diffused blur of light from the window of the sitting room lit up the gravel, a vague gulf of misty rain, a sodden flower bed and a narrow stretch of the sad soaked grass of winter. The light showed that Philipson was at home; Philipson never bothered to draw the curtains; Philipson's ideas of comfort were, in fact, crude; of order, nonexistent.

He and Yorke had been in partnership in a chicken farm for the last two years, and so far the arrangement, if a trifle uneasy at times, had been on the whole fairly satisfactory. They had not known each other before; the least opulent of Yorke's aunts had known a nephew of Philipson's cousin, that was all. But Mark Yorke had some money, and his family thought he needed an occupation; Philipson had a good deal less money, needed to make more, and had some experience of the business.

Their first meeting had taken place, at Philipson's suggestion, in a tea-shop at Farley. When Yorke's aunt transmitted to him the message making the assignation he had lifted eyebrows and shoulders.

"Is he that sort of chap? Oh I say, Aunt!"

"What sort?" his aunt replied vaguely, and like Pilate, did not stay for an answer. She had not the slightest interest in this project of Mark's parents, nor did she care into which category the unknown Mr. Philipson should be inserted. "I dare say he is—I really don't know. I've never seen him. But that was the message—'three-thirty at the Peascod in Peter Paul Street.' "

"The Peascod!" Yorke groaned. "All right."

If he had been pressed to go, Yorke would have utterly refused, and the matter would have come to a full stop. But his aunt's indifference gave no scope for perversity. He went to the Peascod on the day appointed, though not at three-thirty. He was not going to sit waiting in a tea-shop, looking a fool, till the other fellow turned up. He therefore arrived at four-ten. Mr. Philipson, a girl in a green overall told him, had booked a table by phone, but he had not come yet. Yorke sat down; he would just see at what time the man did come.

A little after four-thirty, Philipson arrived. He looked untidy and fretful, but not as if he were in a hurry, and he did not apologize.

If he had apologized it would have been an end of the acquaintance, but, to Yorke, there was something so large in the fellow's discourtesy that he was positively impressed. Before they parted that afternoon he had agreed to try what he alluded to as "the parents' rustic idea."

Philipson, who believed that he had appointed four-thirty as the hour of meeting, was entirely unconscious of the impression he had created. When he joined Yorke at Miller's Green he did nothing to maintain it, and for several weeks the fate of the partnership hung by a frayed thread, for each man contrived to annoy the other. If Philipson's untidiness exasperated, Yorke's insistence on order seemed to Philipson nothing short of spinsterish. Yorke despised his partner's utter ordinariness; Philipson was riled at Yorke's conscious superiority. "Blasted young snob," he called him in his own mind.

But, after a time, and by fits and starts, the two began to find out a number of surprising things about each other. Philipson had not expected that the elegant young man with the smoothly waved hair, whose talk, when it was not of Sir This and Lady That, was of bridge, or literature, or private theatricals, would prove to have an excellent head for figures, and far more business ability than he had himself; though that, indeed, was not saying much.

Yorke's great discovery with regard to his partner was even more startling, and quite fortuitous. A casual reference of Philipson's to Paris might have led to it in the first week of their joint housekeeping at Miller's Green, but it did not. Yorke had lifted his eyebrows at the mention of Paris, and remarked, but it was really not a question that desired an answer: "Oh! You've been there, have you?"

"Once———" Philipson began, and stopped. He had intended to say, "Once I thought of settling down there," but, conscious that his past life was his own, and not Yorke's business, he shut his mouth and said no more.

"I suppose," said Yorke, "that half the population of the south of England goes over now on these weekend tickets."

Philipson said he supposed so. Whether or not he realized Yorke's misapprehension, he did not correct it, and the subject did not come up again till several weeks later.

But one day Philipson had mislaid a letter (no uncommon occurrence) containing a quotation for incubators, and Yorke, decidedly out of temper, was standing over him while he ferreted among the contents of his perpetually untidy desk. Empty envelopes, several pencils, some crossed and rusted nibs, a few letters, and a box of drawing pins, dislodged by the frenzied search, had fallen and now lay spread about the floor. Yorke bit his lip in vexation. He knew his partner well enough by now to be sure that, if any one picked them up, it would not be Philipson.

As the lower strata of the desk's contents were reached a sketch book toppled out to join the other things: a sheet from a sketching block followed it, and lay face upwards.

Upon the sheet was a rough charcoal sketch of a feather, a single feather from a heron's wing. The drawing was nothing more than a hint, hastily dashed off, but the few sure and lively lines recorded and revealed a thing so light as to ride the air, yet strong with the strength of the long slow wingbeats.

Yorke scooped the paper up from the floor and stood staring at it. Philipson, pulling out another drawer, disturbed a fresh avalanche of papers, but Yorke did not notice them.

"This is good," he said.

Philipson was peering into the space behind the drawer. He did not answer.

"Who did it?"

Philipson turned round.

"Oh! that?" He took it out of Yorke's hand, and looked at it upside down. "Oh! yes. I'd forgotten that." He looked about for somewhere to put it, and rammed it carelessly into a pigeon-hole.

Yorke repeated, with asperity: "It's *good*. Who did it?"

As though Yorke had focused Philipson's notice upon the sketch for the first time, he pulled it out again and stared at it.

"That was at Vernon," he muttered, remembering the heat of the September day, the flash of sunshine on the river, and the spattered light and shadow through the woods that muffled the steep, winding Gisors road. "I did it." His voice added: "Of course."

He shoved it back again. "I can't find that damn' thing anywhere," he complained bitterly.

But Yorke's craving for information on the subject of incubators had been superseded by another curiosity.

"Can I look at your sketch book?" he asked.

"Oh yes," Philipson pushed it towards him with his foot. "If you like."

Yorke did like. He sat down and looked through it carefully and slowly. No craftsman could resist such attention. Before long Philipson came and sat beside him; then went upstairs and fetched untidy parcels done up with tape, or string, or bootlaces. Yorke untied every one, and went through the contents with the same absorbed interest. It was surprising, but it was undoubtedly true, that this insignificant, harassed-looking fellow, with his bush of prematurely grey hair and his entirely prosaic conversation, was a very creditable worker in wood and lino-cuts, with a technique of portraiture that was more than an amateur's.

After that, in spite of Yorke's fastidiousness, and Philipson's nervous irritability, the two rubbed along pretty well. Yorke had plenty of social engagements to take him out of the house, and his sincere admiration for the older man's work helped him to overlook what he did not like. Philipson, for his part, grew accustomed to Yorke's "highfalutin" as he called it to himself, and certainly the financial advantages of the partnership were considerable.

Yorke came abreast of the window, and stood still looking in; his feet had made no noise upon the grass verge of the path; he could watch, if he chose, like the onlooker at a play, whatever was going on inside.

And the room had indeed that peculiarly unreal, theatrical air which a lit interior presents to any one looking in from the dark outside. It was perhaps the fascination of this strange aspect of familiar things which kept Yorke standing there; or perhaps it was the slight sense of power which comes sometimes to an unseen watcher. His eyes took in, as if he had never seen it before, the go-as-you-please, easy comfort of the long, low-ceilinged room. His own bookshelves faced him, slim modern poets jostling the square John-Bullish shoulders of nineteenth century novelists. There was a pile of magazines on the gate-legged table, and a Chinese bowl which he had picked up in a back street near Victoria. In the corner by the fireplace Philipson's desk boiled over with a mixture of accounts, poultry catalogues, pencil sketches, and lino-blocks. Yorke's own desk, irreproachably neat, stood in the opposite corner.

One of the really outsize easy chairs which Yorke had imported, contained Philipson, invisible except for his legs in those grey slacks which were, Yorke thought, very suitable for the hen houses, but not so proper for dinner; but Philipson didn't seem to distinguish between occasions. Yorke's eyes fastened themselves now on the slacks, and on the shoes that ended them. As usual Philipson's left leg was crossed over his right, and swung restlessly with an occasional nervous jerk.

"Why can't he keep still!" Yorke muttered. The swinging foot fascinated and infuriated him. He could not bear it any longer. He stepped over the path, and rapped smartly on the window.

The result would have been immensely gratifying to a schoolboy. Like a dog startled out of sleep, Philipson came up out of the chair head and feet at once, while the book he had been reading flew through the air and fell face downward on the floor. Philipson's face, a mask of fear, stared blindly at the blank dark of the window. Yorke could not help laughing. But, as he went on along the path to the front door, and put out his hand to the big black iron ring knocker, he was frowning. What on earth was up with his partner?

When Mrs. Harker let him in, Yorke went straight upstairs, and in a bath, that solvent of so many cares, he almost forgot Philipson's strange behaviour. But Philipson himself had not forgotten. Yorke found him, not lounging as usual, full length in his chair, but sitting on the edge of it, his chin on his fist, his elbow upon the book which he had retrieved from the floor, and which now, its pages badly dog-eared, was laid face downwards on his knee. Yorke knew that it was only a sixpenny shocker, but for him a book, however cheap or bad, was a book, and such treatment pained him.

"You startled me." Philipson accompanied the superfluous statement with what he meant for a laugh but it was a bad imitation.

Yorke was not a young man who usually took much interest in other people; he found himself too absorbing for that; but tonight he did realize that it was strange that Philipson, instead of being as cross as a bear because Yorke had startled him, seemed inclined almost to apologize for being startled.

"I was reading a thriller," Philipson added, and backed that up by holding the book out for Yorke to read the title.

Yorke read it; he made no comment, but his expression said: "What tripe!" When Philipson rather pointedly settled himself again in the chair, and lifted the book, he got up and

went over to the bookshelves. The despised thriller had reminded him of something of a different calibre. When he
came back to the fire he had in his hands Poe's "Tales"; he
turned over the pages till he found that story of "The Pur-
loined Letter," the thesis of which, fantastic but convincing,
is that the way to hide a thing is to put it in the most ostentatiously visible place.

It is undeniably a good story, and Yorke appreciated not
only that, but the style of the telling; yet, as he read his attention wandered, and his eyes, leaving the page, would rest on
Philipson sprawling opposite him, the book in one hand, the
other fidgeting with a loose button on his coat, and his foot
swinging and jerking in the very same way that had so annoyed Yorke half an hour before.

What had Philipson been doing that afternoon? That was
the question. Well, he would find out.

"Had a bad time at the dentist's?" he asked suddenly.

Philipson's head jerked back. "What? No, not so—— As a
matter of fact—— Well rather. Yes, it did rather upset me."

"Sorry," said Yorke. He saw that Philipson was growing
restive under his eyes, so he looked down at Poe's "Tales"
again. But after a moment:

"What time was your appointment?"

"Two-forty-five," Philipson was curt. "Why do you want
to know?"

"No reason in particular. I was in Mallingford this afternoon; sold off at the Market earlier than I expected, so I
came back through there and went to the Veres's. But I could
have picked you up and brought you home if I'd known."

Philipson did not acknowledge Yorke's amiability with anything more than a grunt. Only after a moment he added, with
an obvious effort: "I got the bus back."

Yorke nodded, and returned to his book. After all Philipson was a queer old bird, and if he'd had a bad time at the
dentist's—— York decided that the explanation was sound
enough, and put the matter out of his mind. After a moment
he laid down his book and reached up to the chimney piece

for his pipe. When he had filled and lit it he turned again to Philipson.

The thriller did not seem to be very absorbing. At Yorke's slight movement Philipson slapped it down on his knee. "What is it now?" he cried in an exasperated voice.

"I was going to tell you what I did at Farley, at market, I mean."

"Oh! Well, go on."

Yorke was not to be discouraged. Not only did he give a full account of all the business done, but, when that ground was covered he went on to recount his doings for the rest of the day: lunch at the Mitre with an old school friend—a very amusing lunch, according to Yorke; then back to Mallingford —"I meant to go straight to the Veres's for a spot of bridge, but the old bus wanted air, so I left her at Peppard's."

He paused to knock out his pipe on the hearth. Then he turned again to Philipson. Philipson was drumming with his fingers on the back of his book; his aspect did not, as did the eyes of Anne Boleyn, "invite to conversation." Yorke, however, who could be a very good talker when he liked, bore on. If he chose to give Philipson an account of his doings, give it he would.

"So," he continued, "while he coped with it, I went up to Endicott's about those cockerels, but he was out. And I came back by Marshall's farm, but old Marshall was out—at least I couldn't make any one hear. Suppose they'd both gone to market. I wanted to see if I could do anything about those pullets he owes us for." He stopped because Philipson had knocked his book off his knee. Yorke was watching him as he fumbled with it, and at last picked it up.

"Have you been over to Marshall's lately, Philipson?"

Philipson did not jump this time. He stuffed the book firmly between his knee and the chair. "No," he said, and let the blank negative stand.

"Shocking bad state the place is in," Yorke ran on. "I shouldn't wonder if the old blackguard isn't pretty nearly bankrupt. Thatch all moss where it isn't holes, gutters dripping, stink of rats in the kitchen—ugh! Not that I went in today. As I said, the old boy was out, everywhere shut up. I didn't even see the lady you admire so much."

Philipson said, with a kind of jerk: "Where did you go next?"

"No, but just tell me," Yorke brought him back to the point he had evaded: "What is it that you see in her? I think she's deuced plain."

"Well," for a minute Philipson's eyes lost a look of strain that had been in them since Yorke had begun to talk; he seemed now to be contemplating something both distant and satisfying. "Well, she's got a most unusual shaped face for one thing. And hardly any colour, almost a monotone, and then those long eyebrows, and the long mouth, repeating the curve, you see. And the black pupils in the pale eyes."

Yorke laughed, not very pleasantly.

"I've heard all that before, when you were painting her. 'But this I know not, whence thief's eyes have come into our race.'"

"What?" Philipson looked blank.

"That," said Yorke, "is from *The Story of Burnt Njal*. It's not your sort of book, but it's a masterpiece."

"Oh," Philipson made no effort to pursue the conversation, either on the subject of Mrs. Marshall or of Icelandic literature. He picked up his paper-backed thriller, and began, rather obviously, to find his place in it. When Yorke, in argumentative tone, remarked that "if he were the old man he wouldn't trust Mrs. Marshall a yard," Philipson did not ostensibly hear, but made some parade of turning over a page.

For a few minutes Yorke left him alone. He picked up one of the library books he had brought back from Farley. It was a book of recent Oriental travel. Yorke flipped over the pages, looking more or less perfunctorily at the illustrations. But palm trees, donkeys, deserts, sun-smitten mosques could not hold his attention; he did not even seem to care if he saw the palm trees growing horizontally rather than vertically, and when he had run through the book once, he let it drop back onto the rug and, getting out of his chair, began to prowl restlessly about the room.

Philipson read on, but it was with difficulty, and now and again he raised his eyes to scowl at Yorke's straight and beautifully tailored back.

If he had not been in his black mood he might have found something to enjoy in watching the younger man, for Yorke had good looks, and what is more he had grace—not only the athelete's grace, though he was a good fencer, a more than passable shot, and a very pretty bat—but the grace of action that trained actors, and some lucky amateurs have. As he moved about the room, running his fingers along the backs of his books, shuffling some papers on his desk, parting the curtains to look out at the dripping dark, he was never for a moment clumsy. A young lady, an admirer of his, and an intellectual, had once in a poem likened his movements to "quick, supple, wind-blown flame"; the phrase had pleased her, and indeed it was nearer to the truth than much poetry. Yorke was unusually satisfying to watch.

He was, for all that, intensely annoying to Philipson, who at last giving up all pretence of reading, clapped the book down on his knee and demanded why the devil he couldn't sit still, and what was the matter with him this evening?

Yorke, prowling behind Philipson's chair, pulled up, and looked down at the thick bush of Philipson's grey hair. Philipson's small, knotty hand came up and began tousling it irritably. He gave it a good jerk, muttered "Damn" with some feeling, touched the side of his head very gingerly, and looked quickly round at Yorke.

"Well, you see," said Yorke, "as a matter of fact, I suppose I must be a bit worked up tonight. This afternoon the other side of Achester I nearly smashed up the old bus and projected myself—and that at about fifty miles an hour, into Abraham's bosom. Bit of a shock for the Patriarch it would have been."

He came round from behind Philipson and dropped again into his own chair.

"You know, Philipson," he said. "It's danger, I'm sure it's danger, that makes you really taste life. I—I could jump over the moon tonight." He gave a little laugh, with apology in it, and yet there was more of excitement. Philipson's face remained blank, but Yorke persisted. "Don't you think so? I mean about danger? Not about the moon.

"I'll tell you what," he went on after a ruminative pause, "the difference between you and me—" he broke off, and grinned at Philipson's averted face. "One of the differences, I mean, is that you're an artist of the sensuous, the material. But I'm an artist of sensation, feeling, experience. If"—he gave a little laugh—"Yes. If I were going to be hanged I'd be interested in what I was feeling about it."

Philipson moved restlessly in his chair. It made him feel uncomfortable when Yorke talked as if he, Philipson, were a literary society. And the word sensuous made him uneasy too, being associated in his mind with things not quite respectable.

"Well, then"—Yorke, having secured his audience, did not wish to lose its attention—"Then, I mean after Peppard had finished with the car, I went on to the Veres's. It was such a beastly afternoon that they were all in, and their tongues lolling out for a game of bridge. I suspect that the girls lost a pot of money at Monte last month. You could see them rolling up their sleeves and stropping the knife when I blew in. So we settled down to a good three hours of it—yes, it must have been quite as long as that. They're damn' good players too, sharp as mustard, but today," again Yorke laughed, and again with that note of tension and excitement, "but today I guess my luck was in, and I won close on a fiver from them." He reflected a minute, his eyes on the fire, then: "Do you believe in luck, Philipson?"

"In bad luck—I do."

The morose conviction of his partner's tone only seemed to amuse Yorke. "Oh, come!" he remonstrated laughing, "but it's the other sort I mean. And I believe my luck's in."

Philipson took immediate advantage of a pause to lift his book pointedly; but such a barrage was nothing to Yorke. Philipson heard him chuckle, but did not look up; next instant the young man was off again.

"Why are policemen so funny?" he asked.

"Are they?"

"Of course they are. Look at the old pantomime. Look at all the jokes."

Philipson, though unwillingly, contributed to the conversation the suggestion that perhaps they weren't funny to criminals.

"I don't know so much; they may be—screamingly funny. But we can't know, since we're neither of us in that line of business. Anyway, as I was going to tell you, I picked up our respected Sergeant Tucker as I came back from the Veres's, and gave him a lift as far as the gate. You'll be glad to hear that he's satisfied with the morals and general deportment of Benmarsh. In fact he even gave me to understand that if he'd any craving for glory he'd need a few nice juicy——"

Just what would have been the desiderata of Sergeant Tucker, Philipson was not to learn. That moment the telephone exploded with the personal virulence peculiar to some of those instruments.

3

PEPPARD SAYS: "INDEED!"

PHILIPSON DAMNED THE thing venomously as he
rolled out of his chair and shambled across the
room. But when he had picked up the receiver and listened
for a second, his expression changed from irritation to astonishment, from astonishment to dismay. As the conversation
proceeded, with Yorke listening like the spectator at a play,
his face gradually cleared to something approximating to a
rather embarrassed cheerfulness.

"Oh! I say . . . Oh! Sir, I'm sorry. What? Yes, I'm afraid
I had. I . . . I can't think how I came to . . . to . . . Can
I? But I'm . . . Doesn't it matter? Just as I am? I'll be there
in two twos . . . Right. It is good of you . . . But I am so
. . . Right. Good-bye."

He banged down the receiver and turned to Yorke.

"I shan't be in to dinner. I'm going to the Vicarage. You
might tell Mrs. Harker, will you?" He was halfway to the
door with something far more brisk in his manner than he
had shown this evening.

Yorke, who sometimes indulged in an almost feminine
curiosity, asked: "Had you forgotten?"

Philipson stopped with his hand on the door. He turned
slowly round to Yorke, and the expression of his face was hard
to understand. Was it, Yorke asked himself, sullen or fright-

ened—but then why frightened?—or was it simply angry?

"Any one can forget—a thing like that," he said, and shut the door behind him.

He had not been gone five minutes when the phone rang again. Yorke let it ring for a minute; then he got up and went to it with not much more enthusiasm than Philipson had shown.

"This is Morgan speaking—" came the distant, attenuated voice. "Can I speak to Mr. Philipson?"

"He's out," Yorke answered shortly. Who the devil was Morgan? Oh! Philipson's dentist. Philipson had been to the dentist this afternoon. "This is his partner speaking," he added. "Can I give him a message?"

Mr. Morgan thought, and said, that that was very kind of Mr. Yorke. He had only once before spoken to Philipson's partner, and had not, on that occasion, found him so helpful.

"Could you? Thanks, then. Well, will you ask him if I'm to book another appointment for him?" Even through the phone the voice sounded aggrieved. "He didn't turn up this afternoon."

Yorke had opened his mouth to yawn, but he shut it quickly. "It's very inconvenient, Mr. Yorke," said the voice in his ear, "when patients don't keep their appointments. Though I expect, of course, that Mr. Philipson couldn't help it."

"Yes, I expect so. I'll tell him. Good night."

Yorke took the receiver from his ear, and Mr. Morgan's thanks and farewells dwindled to a faint squeak, and were quenched.

So Philipson hadn't been to the dentist this afternoon. Yorke went back to the fireplace but he did not sit down. Instead, he stood staring into the flames and now and again poking the coals with the toe of his shoe. If Philipson hadn't been to the dentist, where had he been? And had it something to do with his undeniably queer behaviour this evening? Yorke told himself that he was a fool to worry. It couldn't be anything—that mattered. But "I'll try and find out something from Mrs. Harker," he said to himself.

He had not to seek an opportunity. It was Agnes, the daily maid, who announced dinner, but when Yorke went into the dining room he found Mrs. Harker standing by the sideboard. That did not surprise him; he was not given to noticing who served him, so long as he was well served. But in reality Mrs. Harker's presence in the dining room was of some significance. Had Mr. Philipson been in to dinner it would have been Agnes who waited on the two men; when Mrs. Harker learned from "the girl"—Agnes was not often allowed the dignity of a name—that Mr. Yorke was alone, she hastily took off her enormous cook's apron, and girded herself with something, still austerely old-fashioned, but more in keeping with the temporary office of a parlourmaid. If Mr. Yorke, whom she always referred to as "the master," was alone, Mrs. Harker would seize the opportunity of a tête-à-tête with the god of her idolatry.

For Mrs. Harker, elderly, horse-faced, and domineering, with her perpetual, recurrent sniff and her odd pattering walk, which looked, Yorke said, as if she were wearing bananas on her feet, was, like many another hard nut, a sentimentalist, and Mr. Yorke, a "toff" and the friend of "toffs"—Mrs. Harker's word—was her ideal. Sublimely oblivious to the convenience, sometimes apparently to the very existence of servants, except on some occasions when a capricious fancy seized him to be irresistibly confidential with them about his own affairs—(this would happen when he could not find any other audience)—he was a master whom she was proud to serve. When he wore evening dress, and an eyeglass with a broad, black, and piquantly feminine ribbon, Mrs. Harker felt that "those Socialists" had not yet succeeded in their wicked and foolish designs; there were still *some* gentlemen left. By comparison with Mr. Yorke, Mr. Philipson, whose mood and method wavered between the apologetic and the fretful, suffered much.

Tonight, though Mr. Yorke wore a pale grey lounge suit instead of the ritual black and white, Mrs. Harker could have found it in her heart to go down on her knees on the old Shirvan prayer rug before him. For he was in a mood which one of his circle at Oxford, but hardly one of his friends, had once rather unkindly termed "winsome."

"Something good for dinner? It smells jolly good."

Mrs. Harker replied in a properly colourless voice that she hoped so, sir, and offered, as to one of the old gods, a fillet of the sacrificial bull.

"Wizard!" said Mr. Yorke.

Mrs. Harker had supplied him with vegetables, had inquired if he would take wine, had produced instead the whisky and soda which Mr. Yorke preferred, and had gone back to her post at the sideboard, where she stood, in general, as silent and aloof as any weather-beaten stone image. But tonight she broke her silence with a faint apologetic cough.

"If you please, sir, excuse me, but did Mr. Philipson say anything about the honey?"

"Honey? No."

Mrs. Harker's sniff conveyed a wordless but unmistakable criticism of Mr. Philipson's character.

"What about it?"

"Then, sir, I'm afraid, there won't be any for your breakfast."

"Damn!" said Yorke, who did not like marmalade.

"Well, sir," Mrs. Harker spoke in the voice of an early Christian martyr, accused of secret and unmentionable practices, but innocent of all. "Well, sir, I done my best, for I asked him to call and remind them about it, and he said he would and I couldn't do more than that."

"Ring up about it then."

"I can't, sir. We gets it from Joe Parsons."

"Oh!" Yorke was entirely vague.

"Marshall's man, sir, from Oldners Farm."

"Oh!" said Mr. Yorke again, but this time not vaguely. "Then——" he stopped, hesitating how to put his question, but Mrs. Harker spared him the trouble.

"And you see, sir, when I heard that Mr. Philipson was going to Mallingford this afternoon, I asked him if he was walking would he call at Marshall's and ask Joe to send his little girl round with it."

Mr. Yorke was frowning at his empty plate. For a minute he said nothing, and when he spoke it was to tell Mrs. Harker, rather curtly, that he was ready.

But when she came back with the cheese soufflé he re-opened the conversation.

"Didn't Mr. Philipson call then, Mrs. Harker? At Oldners Farm, I mean."

Mrs. Harker, encouraged, was only too glad to relieve her feelings.

"Well, sir, this afternoon the honey didn't come and didn't come, and so when I heard Mr. Philipson come in, he went straight upstairs, and he was a long time there, and here was I waiting about and not able to get on with my work, and Tuesday such a busy day always as it is. And I didn't hear him come down after all, but after a bit, I'd just answered the door to the bread boy, and I thought surely Mr. Philipson must be down by now, and so I went into the sitting room, and he was, though when he'd come down I couldn't say, though I was listening. And I asked him whether they were sending it, and he said sending what, and I said the honey, and he said damn the honey. And he banged the lid of that bureau of his, because he was sitting by it, but how was I to know that he was that busy, and I don't believe he was, only messing about among all those untidy papers and things that he keeps there. And excuse me for taking the liberty," Mrs. Harker added, with a misgiving that perhaps she had gone too far in her indictment of Mr. Philipson.

Mr. Yorke did not seem to notice that aspect of the question.

"But didn't Philipson go to the farm?" he asked again.

This time Mrs. Harker answered the repeated inquiry. But the answer was that she didn't know. All she could say, and she said it several times, was that Mr. Philipson had started off in plenty of time to go there, "because I saw him go out of the gate, and he had a brown paper parcel under his arm. And more than that I can't say."

"Just as well," thought Yorke, "—if only it were true." But Mrs. Harker was off again.

Yorke, however, had no compunction in making it quite clear that he had had enough. Mrs. Harker withdrew in a chastened silence, but still thrilling with the rare joy of self-expression.

Yorke was left alone to brood upon the increasing obscurity of the question as to what Philipson had been doing in the afternoon.

Meanwhile Philipson, who had started out so briskly for the Vicarage was, after all, not enjoying himself. Indeed, even before he got there, the cloud which had for the moment lifted from his spirits, settled down more heavily than ever. In the great cavern of the Vicar's pseudo-Gothic porch, he told himself, as he heard the jangling echoes of the bell, that he ought never to have come.

Consequently, when Justina herself opened the door to him, Philipson was at his worst and most awkward. His "How d'you do, Miss Tellwright? How are you?" was hurried out in the voice of an uncomfortable and apprehensive stranger. He next made a perfunctory remark about the weather, and laughed, as though he had said, or at least tried to say, something funny. Then, in a strained silence he followed her into the sitting room.

It was as if he had gone back to the earliest day of their acquaintance, to that highly comic but very uncomfortable first visit of his. On that occasion Justina, at home after an exacting case, and revelling in breakfast in bed, unlimited novels, and complete freedom from the necessity of the nurse's tact, had implored her father not to bring in again "that absurd little man" while she was at home. Since those days, the acquaintance, so unpropitiously begun, had much improved. Instead of arduously attempting to cover up Mr. Philipson's *gaffes* with hasty small talk, Justina took care to point them out to him, and his "party manners" were a standing joke, and only one of many.

Today, however, Justina made no jokes. Sensible girl as she was, at Mr. Philipson's inexplicably nervous demeanour she felt something in her flutter and shrink in a perturbation that was not altogether unpleasant. But, because she was sensible, and as nice a girl as you could meet in a long summer day, she took no notice of it in her mind. Laboriously, conscientiously, she tried to make conversation with the guest.

"Someone called to see Dad. I hope they won't keep him."

Mr. Philipson mumbled something; what it was even he himself did not really know.

"They always do manage to come at mealtimes."

Mr. Philipson laughed awkwardly.

"I'm sorry you've got to wait for your supper."

They both found that an unfortunate remark, for both remembered that Mr. Philipson had made no apology for the fact that supper was already half an hour late, entirely owing to his forgetfulness.

Justina, beginning to be a little nettled, thought: "Well, let him apologize. He ought to." But he did not, and she was driven by her social conscience to try again.

"I do hope," she said, "that he isn't stuffing up Dad with some awful tale of woe. Dad will believe almost anything, you know. At least, he never will say he doesn't believe; he thinks it would be so awful for the other fellow to have his word doubted."

Justina, after her hospital training and three years' experience of nursing, was convinced, on the one hand that her father was in this world as a sheep among wolves, on the other that she herself had little left to learn about human depravity. It would have surprised her to be told that she did, in fact, credit all her friends and acquaintances with her own honest candour and her own unquestioning code—or rather, it would have surprised her to hear that to do so was, in some cases, an error in judgment.

"He's being a long time," she said, after another stretch of silence.

Mr. Philipson tried to clear his throat, failed, and muttered hoarsely and hastily that there was no hurry, that it didn't matter, that he meant to say—and left it unsaid.

"Won't you smoke?" Justina asked.

Mr. Philipson pulled out his pipe and filled it, scattering more than a usual amount of tobacco on the carpet.

"Who is it?" he wrenched out.

The effort, tardy though it was, deserved a better reward. Justina did not know who it was. That killed the already moribund conversation, and they sat in silence, neither looking at the other.

Yet Justina was pleasant to look at, without being in the slightest degree a pretty girl. Plump now in her early twenties, she would be definitely, comfortably, graciously fat at forty. Her round face, with a nose almost absurdly snub, and a cheerfully decisive mouth, was sprinkled all over with a thick dusting of freckles. Her voice was the most memorable thing about her; it was low in tone, and its note of authority was softened by a most ridiculous and, if you liked Justina, a delicious drawl. Most people did like Justina.

The silence had lasted unbroken for five minutes when Mr. Tellwright came in; they welcomed him with something of the fervour of castaways upon an inconvenient and badly stocked desert island.

Who, Justina clamoured, had been with him in the study?

"That was Peppard," the Vicar told her.

"Oh! Peppard? I thought it was some creature with a long tale of woe. What did Peppard say?"

Mr. Tellwright, with a glint of gentle amusement replied: "He said 'Indeed.' "

It was a Vicarage joke. Justina laughed.

"How many times? Did you manage to count?" She turned, quite naturally now, to Mr. Philipson who was looking blank.

"Haven't you noticed how Peppard always says 'Indeed'?"

"Only to things that aren't in his left-wing 'daily,' " Mr. Tellwright amended. He smiled at Philipson. "They're all true, but he doubts everything else; or thinks there is some antisocial evil hidden in it."

"Yes, but Dad," Justina persisted, "how many tonight?"

The Vicar began to count on his fingers.

"Let me see. Three times when I was explaining to him that it is not by reason of any personal fad of mine that notices for elections to the Parish Council are put up on the board in the churchyard. Once when I said that the wireless is prophesying fog. And once in the hall. He picked up Philipson's hat by mistake, and I said 'I think that one is Mr. Philipson's' and he said 'Mr. Philipson's? *In*deed.' I couldn't tell whether he didn't believe you'd got a hat, Philipson, or if he thought you were——"

He paused. "Not quite nice for us to know," Justina suggested.

They were all laughing when Martha knocked and said that supper was ready. At supper Mr. Philipson, if not sparkling, seemed at ease; his apprehensive rigidity softened, he answered Mr. Tellwright's inquiries as to the health of the Miller's Green hens, and even gave Justina an illustration of Mr. Yorke's technique with his eyeglass.

By the time he left, Justina had almost forgotten the discomforts of the first half hour. She followed the two men out into the hall, and while Philipson struggled into his coat, slipped her arm through her father's and leaned against him in a way that reminded Mr. Tellwright of a confiding kitten.

"Dear me!" she said, and laughed, "I meant to ask how you got on with your red herring today."

Philipson's "red herrings"—a joke of homely idiocy—were his *bêtes noires*. Justina was in the habit of trailing one of them across the conversation in order to hear his immediate and vehement reaction to the hated name.

"Which one?"

The Vicar had opened the door and gone out into the darkness of the porch to take a look at the weather.

"Why, the reddest of them. Old Marshall."

Philipson was reaching up to take his hat from the peg. His hand remained raised, but his face turned slowly towards her. For a second, but it seemed far longer, he stared at her in the dim light of the hall. It was the light, she told herself afterwards, that made him look so strange.

"I didn't see him."

He grabbed his hat.

"Good night! Thank you!" He was out in the porch. She heard him say the same to her father, then "Good night," again, already a long way down the drive.

4

SERGEANT TUCKER DRAWS BLANK

SERGEANT TUCKER WAS shaving when the telephone bell rang. With his face surrounded by lather as a very outsize cherub's might be by clouds, he hurried downstairs, drying his hands as he went.

"All right, Mother," he called, "I'll answer it."

"All right, Dad," came Mrs. Tucker's cheerful voice from the kitchen, accompanied by a pleasant sizzling of bacon.

Tucker took up the receiver and held it a little way from from his be-clouded ear.

"Hallo! Yes. Sergeant Tucker speaking. Who? Peppard? Morning, Peppard!" Even over the 'phone the change in Tucker's voice was unmistakable, and Peppard did not miss it. He had no more affection for Tucker than Tucker for him.

"Oh! Disappeared?" Tucker listened with disfavour, picturing at the other end of the line Peppard's quick dark eyes, and his perpetually greasy complexion—though a garage proprietor should be excused a certain amount of grease. "You mean Marshall from Oldners Farm, not Marshall at Mill Bank. Very kind of you to let me know. Since when? Last night only, you think. That doesn't sound very serious." Tucker's tone reduced Peppard's news to an irrelevant triviality. "The Postman told you? And said that Mrs. Marshall's in a great taking? Yes, I'll go along. Thank you. Good-bye. Oh! Who's gone to be with her? Oh! Mrs. Peppard. Very kind of her, I'm sure. Good-bye." Tucker rang off.

"Very kind of you both!" he observerd with bitterness to the plant stand. "Meddlesome gossips, the pair of you," he muttered as he went upstairs again, feeling the lather cooling and pricking on his skin. "I bet Peppard'll want to tell me how to run this business—that is if the old chap doesn't turn up again in a day or two. But," he observed to his own face in the mirror, "I'll keep Master Peppard's nose out of it. This isn't the Cricket Club again." With that incontrovertible statement Sergeant Tucker put the matter momentarily out of his mind.

Oldners Farm lies on a byroad that runs along the gentle lower slopes of the chalk hills, bare here and treeless, neither downland nor valley, an intermediate, negative bit of country, inclined to be dreary except when there is blue sky above noisy with larks, and below green corn springing. This byroad links two main London roads that strike off, widening the angle between them as they climb, from Mallingford on the river. It is a byroad little used, for another runs lower down the slope, parallel with it, and more directly connecting Mallingford with Benmarsh and its surrounding hamlets. Connecting the upper and the lower roads there is a grassy lane, the local "Green Lane" which leaves the lower road about halfway between Mallingford and Benmarsh, and comes out upon the upper less than a hundred yards from Oldners Farm.

But today Sergeant Tucker had no intention of taking Green Lane as a short cut, for in winter, unless after a long and hard frost, the lane was a morass, and this winter had, until this week in February, been unusually mild and open. Weather prophets—the local variety, not those officials retained by the B.B.C.—had for the past month been darkly threatening that "we'll have to pay for this sooner or later," and reminding their audience of years when there was snow at Easter or the Derby. The weather today, though not yet agreeable to their prophecies, was winterly and unpleasant enough, for thick fog hid valley and hills, and made even the dripping tangle of the hedgerows as insubstantial almost as smoke.

Sergeant Tucker, forging slowly along on his bicycle, was however grateful to the fog. At least it enabled him to pass Peppard's garage without being seen and hailed. It was with relief that he left the main road and turned into the lane upon which stood Oldners Farm. But he had forgotten Mr. Peppard. He came suddenly, in the clinging white mist, upon a massive yet brisk form bustling down the lane from the farm. With considerable presence of mind Sergeant Tucker bent his head as though to dive over his handle bars, and trod hard on the pedals. But Mrs. Peppard was quicker.

"Sergeant! Sergeant!" The shrill summons was as little to be ignored as the trump of doom. Sergeant Tucker made a confidential remark to his front wheel, put on his brake, and jumped off. But he did not turn the bicycle; he did not even back it towards Mrs. Peppard, he only waited till she came up with him. Peppard's wife was not much more to his taste than Peppard himself.

Mrs. Peppard began to unload her cargo of news before ever she reached Sergeant Tucker, so that it came out in a breathless jumble of unfinished sentences.

"Oh! that poor creature . . . Oh! such a taking as she . . . Never saw the like in . . . Looking like death and I don't believe as her head had touched the pillow. . . . Sitting by the fire . . . only there wasn't no fire and hadn't been for hours, and the kitchen like a tomb."

Gravely inclining his head from time to time—it was the only contribution to the colloquy which Mrs. Peppard's eloquence allowed him—Tucker stood fidgeting, one foot on his pedal, listening to all this and a good deal more of the same sort. As soon as there was a pause he seized his opportunity.

"Thank you, Mrs. Peppard. Now I must be getting along."

Mrs. Peppard, in the excitement of her harrowing news, had forgotten the Tucker-Peppard feud; she had even been ready to lavish upon the Sergeant, not only the news itself, but

Peppard's sensational theories of the event at Oldners Farm. Such gross insensibility, however, outraged her feelings. Well! if the picture of Mrs. Marshall's desolation and her own motherly solicitude did not move him, she was not going to waste even more succulent material. Yet she could not quite refrain from glancing at it, but obscurely.

"Anyway, *if* you've time after," she said with vinegar in her voice, and her small sharp eyes on Tucker's wooden profile, "you'd better call at the garage and talk to Peppard about it. He might be able to tell you something."

Tucker turned to look at her. If his had been a more expressive countenance it would have registered, as the films say, loathing. As it was, it appeared merely blank.

"Tell me something?" he repeated bitterly. "I've no doubt he would. And then some!"

He allowed no time for a reply. Whatever Mrs. Peppard had to say must have been directed to his broad, receding back.

Yet, when he reached Oldners Farm, Tucker had to admit that for once, as he put it to himself, Mrs. Peppard had told no more than the truth. The forlorn room, the disordered hearth where Mrs. Peppard had kindled a fire without sweeping up the litter of the old, the woman, white-faced and all but dumb—Tucker now saw these things for himself. And here he spent a difficult and unfruitful twenty minutes. For Mrs. Marshall would say nothing except in answer to persistent questioning and, even then, her answers were hardly worth having. The only positive statements she made were that Marshall had been busy in the yard in the early afternoon, and then had come in and started drinking—"Yes. Gin, 'e always kept some." He had got very drunk; he had gone out; he had not come back. She had been alone all night for Joe didn't sleep in, and the girl had gone off two days ago without giving notice. But Mrs. Marshall did not know *when* her husband had gone out—"I was cleaning out a bedroom till it was close on dark"—She did not know where he had gone. She did not know any near relations of his that he would have been at all likely to go to, nor, if such people existed, why he should have chosen to go to them. She did not know if he had had anything on his mind lately—not more than usual, but farming these days is a bad business. She did not know if he had received any upsetting letters lately; she had not noticed anything peculiar in his behaviour; she could not think of any one who would be likely to know of anything that would help Sergeant Tucker. Mentally reviewing the information he had got out of her, the Sergeant decided that the only facts he had obtained were that Marshall had been at home, had got drunk, and gone out. As he left the house he was reflecting, though, after the experience of so many years, without surprise, how cut up women were at losing, even temporarily, a husband, however undesirable.

In the yard, Joe Parsons the cross-eyed handy man at Oldners Farm, and at home proprietor of honeybees, was loading up swedes to feed the cattle. Tucker wagged a finger at him on his way to the gate, and then stopped.

"Morning, Joe!"

Joe leaned upon his fork as Saul on Gilboa upon his spear, and with an expression surely as dejected.

"Morning!"

Sergeant Tucker, looking larger, sprucer, fresher than ever by comparison with Joe, began a conversation by the proper remarks about the weather, the Government, and the Grand National. These subjects disposed of, and all suspicion of urgency eliminated from Joe's mind, the Sergeant waited a minute, and then had his reward.

"An' what d'you think of this?" Joe asked, and tipped his head in the direction of the dumb, stone front of Oldners Farm.

"Ah!" said Sergeant Tucker.

"Nice business, I call it."

Tucker knew too well to take out his notebook again. He did not even look at Joe, but picking out a swede, balanced it on his palm as if it were a show specimen, then tossed it back among the others.

"Marshall sent you into market at Farley yesterday, didn't he?" he asked casually.

"Aye. Said I needn't come back after. He'd do the milking

and that. She did it, I suppose." Again he indicated the house.

"Why didn't he go to market himself?"

If Joe had been a Frenchman, eyes, hands and shoulders would have expressed a half amused, half resentful surprise that any one should expect him to know the answer to that question. Being English, he only shook his head.

"What was he—" The words in Tucker's mind were—"up to." He changed them into something less tendentious. "What was he busy with when you left?"

"Fixing up sceer-crow," Joe's head rolled towards the stable this time.

Well, thought the Sergeant, that's not the sort of job a man would waste his time over if he was thinking of doing a get-away.

"It's up in back field. Saw it 'smorning," Joe added.

"Hm!" said Tucker. That the farmer had finished and set it up before he disappeared was neither here nor there. It would not take long to rig up a scarecrow, so this crumb of fact did little even to fix the time of Marshall's return to the farm and the beginning of his drinking bout. Tucker cast about for another line of inquiry.

"Has he been paying you regular?" he asked.

A dim and evanescent gleam of humour brightened Joe's dull, distrustful eye.

"Or I'd not be here," he said.

Tucker felt that he had exhausted the possibilities of obtaining information at Oldners Farm, for the present at any rate, and must glean in other fields. He brought the interview to an end.

He was just mounting his bicycle in the lane when he heard a car approaching. It passed him slowly with a "toot toot," and he recognized Dr. Manning's first edition Ford. Tucker shouted and waved his hand, and the doctor slowed down.

Here was a very different source of information from those that the Sergeant had been so laboriously tapping. When the doctor shoved his square face out of the battered driving flap Tucker told him the news without comment or circumlocution, and then asked the questions that had been forming in his mind.

Dr. Manning rubbed a thick forefinger along his chin so that the bristles rasped.

"Hm! Well, so far as I know anything about old Marshall—but mind you I've only attended him when he sliced his finger half off in a chaff-cutter—I should say he's a very tough customer mentally and physically. Good for ten years yet, in the ordinary way of things. Heart sound as a bell, and nervous system like an ox. Lose his memory? Not he! Precious few people do genuinely lose their memories, you know. Generally means, when you hear it on the wireless, that the family's trying to 'save face.' Fellow's probably gone off on purpose, and his people know it. I should think old Marshall had too. Unless, of course, he was so dead drunk that he got run down on the road somewhere. I suppose you've tried the hospitals?"

Tucker had, and he had of course notified the police round about, but no one in the least like Marshall had been reported. And now he was going round to see the neighbours, and the landlords of the local pubs.

"Good luck then!" the doctor wished him, but as he drove off Tucker felt that the wish, though kindly meant, was vain. First in the category of neighbours came Peppard, whose garage, set on the main road between Mallingford and Swinbrook, commanded the end of Oldners Lane.

Peppard was there, peering into the open bonnet of a lorry, under what had been the comfortable, red-tiled roof of a smithy in the old days. As he came out to speak to Tucker, he wiped his hand on a rag that could hardly be expected to do more than redistribute the dirt, then stuck it back in the pocket of his boiler-suit.

"Morning!"

"Morning!"

Tucker braced himself.

"I want to ask you a thing or two about this business at Marshalls's."

"Ask away." Peppard's eyes, restless, and so Tucker always suspected, censorious, darted from the Sergeant to his bicycle, to the road beyond, and back to Tucker's face. "Well?"

"I thought," said Tucker, "that as your garage is handy for

the lane, you might have seen Marshall if he came past this way at all yesterday."

"Well, I didn't. Because I wasn't here all the afternoon." His tone put the last sentence into italics.

Tucker ignored them.

"When did you see him last?"

"Sunday. No, Saturday." Peppard smiled, as if to himself, but Tucker ignored that too.

"Your man might have seen him. If he was here."

"You can ask him." Peppard disassociated himself from the business and retired again to the lorry, which he contemplated with the air of one who considers an exhibit in a museum.

Tucker asked his question of Peppard's even dirtier assistant, but Tim had seen nothing of Marshall.

Had he then seen any one else who might have been to the farm and seen Marshall.

Tim ruffled his hair thoughtfully.

"Mr. Yorke left his car here for air. He walked up to Endicott's and back by Marshall's but Marshall wasn't there then."

"Mr. Yorke. What time was that?"

Tim thought it was about three o'clock.

"And did he say Marshall wasn't there then?"

Tim ruffled his hair again, then his face brightened. No, but Mr. Yorke had said that he'd had his walk for nothing.

"Thanks," said Tucker. As he wheeled his bicycle across the pavement he was thinking that the interview had not been so annoying as he had expected. Then he found that Peppard had followed him, and now had laid his oily hand upon the handlebars.

"You think this is a case of disappearance, don't you, Sergeant?"

Tucker said, yes he did, and what else could it be?

"Plenty of things. What about suicide, or—murder?"

Tucker laughed, and took his bicycle firmly from Peppard's grip.

"Oh, so Mr. Yorke's murdered old Marshall, has he?"

"Not Mr. Yorke," said Peppard.

Tucker laughed again.

"Well, you find the body, and then I'll ask you to tell me who did it."

Peppard made no reply, but when Tucker had gone and he and Tim were again poring over the intestines of the lorry, he interspersed his diagnosis of its complaint with very wounding comments upon the effect of authority upon character; on the personnel of the modern police force; upon individual liberty; and upon the iniquity of the capitalist régime. But whatever the subject of his discourse Tim was able to comprehend that its object was Sergeant Tucker.

5

YORKE PROVIDES A CLUE

JUST ABOUT THE time that Sergeant Tucker mounted his bicycle to set off for Oldner's Farm, Mr. Yorke came in to breakfast at Miller's Green. The dining room was a cheerful place, in spite of the glum prospect from the window, out of which, this morning, nothing could be seen but the nearer rose trees, awash with fog, and beyond only a sickly and discoloured blank. But inside the room there was a huge fire, a mingled smell of toast, kipper, and coffee, and on the trivet a plate of Mrs. Harker's famous scones. Mrs. Harker regulated her scones as carefully as the supply of manna in the wilderness; they were never allowed to cloy on the palate. She made them just when she thought fit, and not even Mr. Yorke could have exacted them contrary to her determination. She always had some special reason for their manufacture; today they were a challenge to the fog.

"Scones!" Yorke shut the door upon the word, but it had been heard in the kitchen.

"There!" said Mrs. Harker to Agnes. "That's Mr. Yorke. Now Mr. Philipson—did *he* say anything about them?"

"No, but——"

Mrs. Harker sniffed with emphasis, and Agnes, who, if not

intimidated, might have proved an advocate for Mr. Philipson, swallowed her remark.

"Scones!" said Mr. Yorke again. "Good egg!"

At the table Philipson was already bent over a kipper with the harassed air of one who is shortsighted and hates bones. "I've put yours in the hearth," he said and immediately became absorbed again in an anxious pursuit. "I hate kippers," he said bitterly when he could speak again.

"You begin badly," Yorke told him, slitting up his own, neatly, and raising from it the delicate system of silvery filaments. "Get the big ones out all in one, first, and then, if you find the little ones in your mouth, shut your eyes and swallow them."

Philipson laboured in silence for a moment, then pushed his plate away. "It's not worth the trouble," he concluded. "No thanks," he added, as Yorke pushed along the marmalade, and he began to roll up his napkin.

Yorke looked at him again. "Are you off colour?"

Philipson hesitated. "I had a bad night," he said.

"Yes, you do look rather tuckered up."

"I'm all right." Philipson seemed to find Yorke's stare irritating. He got up quickly, pushed his chair under the table, and made for the door.

"I say!"

He stopped at Yorke's voice, his hand on the knob. "What?"

"Morgan rang up last night. He wants you to ring him."

"Damn!" said Philipson, and then stood, rattling the handle of the door. "Did he say anything else?" he asked after a slight pause.

"No. Just that."

"All right, I'll ring him. Thanks." His relief was obvious. "I'm going to the top field," he said, and went.

It was a few minutes after his departure that Agnes brought in the letters. There were three for Yorke, and one for Philipson.

"Shall I take it to him, sir?" Agnes ventured.

"No, I'll give it him when I go out." Yorke did not see,

and if he had seen, would not have remarked Agnes's expression of disappointment. He was looking through his letters.

When Agnes had gone out, he got up and went over to the fireplace, holding them in his hand. There, toasting his shins, he proceeded to open them. The first, with a typewritten address, was a courtly missive from his London tailors, announcing the approaching visit of their representative to Farley. Yorke stuffed it back into its envelope, and dropped both into the fire. The foreign letter came next. He drew out the thin, faintly crackling sheets; there were many of them. "Golly!" he said to himself, "what reams Constance does produce!"

He put it on the chimney piece and took up the third letter. The envelope was dirty, and addressed in a scrawling, illiterate hand.

Some people have a habit of toying with their correspondence before opening it; especially, if they do not recognize the handwriting, will they try to read the postmark, in the hope that this will give them a clue to the writer. So now Mr. Yorke pored over the envelope, before he slit it expertly with his penknife and took out the letter.

He spread out the single sheet, holding it distastefully with the tips of his fingers. When he had read it he crumpled it up and pitched it into the fire; it bounced out; he stooped, picked it up, rammed it into the hottest flame, and even poked at it savagely when it was nothing but a fluttering blackened thing of delicatest ash. When nothing was left, he gathered up the rest of his correspondence, drank a second cup of coffee standing, and went out of the dining room.

Philipson was rooting for something in the big chest in the hall. Yorke hailed him.

"Here, I say, there's a letter for you." He held it out. "And did you ever hear such damned cheek? That fellow Marshall has written to me asking if I can lend him money. I'll see him in hell first."

Philipson took his letter, looked at it, and stuffed it into his pocket. "Do you know where Ackwood's catalogue was put?" he asked.

That morning Yorke devoted to business letters concerning

the poultry farm. The fog had not lifted, rather it had thickened and deepened in colour, and by now had penetrated even into the rooms. In the unnatural dusk Yorke sat at his desk, his reading lamp alight, on his left an ash tray with a growing heap of stubbed cigarette ends, and on his right a growing heap of letters.

It was close on noon when he heard the click of the garden gate, and the sound of heavy footsteps on the path. Out of the corner of his eye he caught a glimpse of the large, blue-uniformed figure of Sergeant Tucker even before the policeman's determined assault upon the knocker.

After a moment Mrs. Harker's long face appeared at the sitting-room door.

"If you please. sir, it's Sergeant Tucker."

"Oh! What does he want?" Yorke threw a crumpled envelope into the wastepaper basket, and added one more letter to a neat pile on the desk.

"He doesn't say, sir. Only could he speak to you for a few minutes."

"All right," said Yorke. "Show him in."

Mrs. Harker shut the door. Yorke rolled up a wad of papers, slipped a rubber band over the tube, and tucked them into a pigeonhole. He was just getting to his feet when Mrs. Harker showed in the Sergeant.

Sergeant Tucker, when pressed, sat down on the very edge of Philipson's chair, his blue helmet at his feet like a blind man's dog, but he refused a cigarette—"On duty, you know, sir—" he said.

"What is it, Sergeant?" asked Yorke.

Sergeant Tucker was wrestling with a notebook that fitted tightly into his breast pocket. When he had extracted it:

"Well, sir, I've come to ask you if you can give us some information. It's a case, so far as we know, of disappearance."

"Oh! Who's disappeared?"

"Old Marshall, from Oldners Farm. At least it looks like that," Tucker added, with ingrained official caution.

"Really!" Yorke's tone was interested. He jerked his monocle out of his pocket, contorted his face, and let his eye socket swallow and hold the thing. Tucker watched, fascinated. He had not encountered Mr. Yorke's monocle before, and his previous experience of such articles had been limited to those he had seen, mostly as adjuncts of villainy, upon the films. He had to be prodded by another question before he would explain his visit to Miller's Green. Then it seemed he had heard that Mr. Yorke had been at Oldners Farm yesterday afternoon, and he wanted to know whether, if that were correct, he had seen Marshall there.

Yorke shook his head.

"I did go up there, but I didn't see him."

Sergeant Tucker had feared as much, but said he would like to know what had happened.

"Right. Only I'm afraid it won't help you much. My car wanted air—I'd been in to Market at Farley, and I was going on to Tetcot—So I stopped at Peppard's. I suppose it was he that told you I was up at Marshall's?"

Tucker nodded.

"Well, I thought that as I'd have to wait, I'd go up to Endicott's about some corn—and he was out too when I got there—and take the farm on my way back." He hesitated, and then explained: "There's—Marshall owes us something, and I wanted to see him."

Tucker nodded again with complete comprehension.

"When I got to the farm I knocked at the door—it was shut—but no one answered, though I *thought* I could hear someone about in the house, somewhere behind, or upstairs, not in the kitchen."

"Yes," Tucker put in. "Mrs. Marshall was there."

"But surely she'd have heard me?"

Tucker shook his head. "It's a rambling old place and it seems that she was in one of the bedrooms."

"Oh!" said Yorke, "I see. Anyway, I thought that as it was Farley market day they'd probably all gone off there. So I rambled about a bit and looked into the stables and the big barn, just to see if Marshall was anywhere about, and then came away without seeing a soul."

Tucker sat for a few minutes like a pillar of salt, his broad, blunt face furrowed with thought. He didn't enjoy this detective business; it had taken him the whole morning to learn—nothing. He sighed, shut his notebook, and then, doubtfully, opened it again.

"I suppose you wouldn't mind, sir," he said in an apologetic tone, "just telling me, what you did after. Just a formality," he added hurriedly. "In *case* it turns out to be anything—anything not a disappearance."

Yorke looked a little puzzled.

"Why, certainly. Let me see. I drove over to Tetcot as soon as the car was ready, played bridge with the Veres's and got back here about seven."

He fixed his eyes on the top of the Sergeant's head as he bent over his notes. "But you don't think," said Yorke, "that it is anything but a disappearance?"

Tucker did not answer till he had finished writing. Then he shut his book and said, with great decision:

"I do not, sir." He seemed about to say more, then to decide that he had better not; in the end he only remarked, somewhat obscurely, that of course Marshall was a middling queer chap.

Even if Yorke had not been long enough in Benmarsh to know that Tucker meant something quite extreme in the way of peculiarity by "middling" queer, he knew enough of Marshall to understand what the Sergeant was driving at. He lifted an elbow in a significant gesture, while one eyebrow went up in a question.

"Like a fish?" the Sergeant confirmed. "But *I* think he's done a get-away. You and Mr. Philipson aren't the only people he owes money to, not by a long shot."

He slipped the rubber band over his notebook, tucked it into his pocket and heaved himself out of the chair. He thanked Mr. Yorke for his help, but from his preoccupied air, it was evident that the business still sat heavy on his mind.

Yorke saw him out. For a moment after he had shut the door on Tucker and on the encroaching fog he stood there; the hall was almost dark; from the kitchen he could hear the sound of running water, and occasionally Mrs. Harker's voice, much louder and sharper than it ever was in the more genteel regions of the house; then from outside came the click of the gate as Sergeant Tucker shut it after him. That seemed to waken Yorke from a study. In two seconds he was back in the sitting room, and had thrown open the window.

"Sergeant! Sergeant!"

There was a scraping slur of brakes, and the Sergeant's voice came out of the fog.

"Yes, sir."

"Here! Come back a moment will you? I've remembered something."

A dim shape leaned its bicycle against the railings, and materialised upon the path again as the Sergeant. Yorke shut the window and went out to open the front door.

Back in the sitting room once more, Tucker waited to hear why he had been recalled. Mr. Yorke was rummaging in the wastepaper basket, but whatever he was looking for seemed to be buried deep, for he had to turn out on the carpet a great collection of torn papers before he cried—"Yes, here it is," and held out to Sergeant Tucker a crumpled and dirty envelope addressed in a scrawling hand.

"I got that this morning," he explained, "but I didn't think of it when we were talking. It's from Marshall. I'm afraid I burnt the letter." Yorke laughed, as if he were a little embarrassed. "I was angry, because the old chap wrote trying to borrow money. I don't know if the envelope will be any use at all."

Sergeant Tucker took the bit of paper, smoothed it out upon one big palm, and brooded over it for a moment.

"Well, the postmark's clear anyhow," he said.

He pointed to it, and Yorke, who had come closer, mounted his monocle again, and bent over the paper with interest.

"Yes. 'February 2nd, 7:30 P.M.!' What's M-a-l-l- . . . ? Oh! of course, 'Mallingford.' "

"Must be," said the Sergeant, without enthusiasm. "But that doesn't tell us much, only that he was there between the seven-thirty collection and the five o'clock; that is if he posted the letter himself. But I've tried the pubs he used to go to, and they say he wasn't there at all last night. And no one saw him at the station either."

He folded up the envelope and began to tuck it into his notebook, but his movements were slow, and his countenance ·

full of gloom. A disappearance, he knew, meant a heap of trouble. Nasty, vague business, a disappearance; nothing to go on, and as likely as not nothing to worry about. But if you didn't worry, and it turned out to be something serious, then you got your tail twisted. And in any case there was the talk and trouble in the village. Tucker's foreboding soul all but groaned aloud. It was so surcharged that he could no longer contain himself, but sought relief in confidences.

"I don't mind telling you, sir, that I really could wish old Marshall at the bottom of the sea—so long as we could prove that he was there all right. It's not only the 'super' and the bigwigs at Farley. It's Benmarsh. You'd be surprised what can happen to a story when people get gossiping. It starts at one end of the street, and its own mother wouldn't know it by the time it gets to the other. And then the clues they bring you! Wanting you to search here, and search there. Not that we take action on hearsay, but when we don't they sometimes get that unpleasant!" Tucker paused, tried to recapture his official taciturnity, and failed. "And here's Peppard already," he ran on, "with a bee in his bonnet about someone having done the old chap in, and wanting me to look for a murderer."

Yorke looked a little startled, but Tucker snorted with scorn. "In Benmarsh!" he said.

Yorke laughed. "Not very likely," he said. "I should think old Marshall——"

He stopped so sharply that Tucker stared at him.

"I say," Yorke went on, "I say, look here. It may be all bunkum, but when you said. . . . Of course there may be nothing in it. . . ."

Even the most jealous practitioner would have been disarmed by such an unassuming amateur. Sergeant Tucker beamed on the young man much as a proud nurse upon a towardly but diffident child about to recite to company.

"Yes sir?" he threw in encouragingly.

"Well," Yorke went on, but still with some hesitation, "when you said about the bottom of the sea—I suppose that put it into my mind. I mean, if Marshall did get some more to drink at Mallingford—perhaps he went to a friend's house, you know—and if he started to go home across the fields he'd have to pass by Pilly's Pond, and if he were pretty tight——"

"There's a white rail," said the Sergeant.

"True. Yes. Of course." Yorke's tone withdrew his motion, but Sergeant Tucker hit one palm with the other fist.

"Yes, sir, but I believe you've got it. If Marshall was blotto that rail wouldn't stop him, and once in, he'd not be likely to get out. The bank's steep there."

With sudden and decisive energy he pushed his notebook back into his pocket, and slapped it smartly; he had the air of a man who is, after a long and painful doubt, resolved upon action.

"I'll get the grapnel this afternoon, and some men to help, and we'll drag that pond."

Yorke followed him to the door. In the hall the Sergeant asked: "Would you come and help, sir? And Mr. Philipson, if it wouldn't be too much trouble. I want people who won't talk afterwards."

"I'll come certainly, if I can be of any use," Yorke told him. "I can't answer for Philipson."

The Sergeant stepped out into the fog again, but with such patient cheerfulness that he felt called upon to correct a possible false impression.

"Of course," he said, "I hope he'll turn up somewhere alive."

"Yes indeed, I hope so," replied Yorke politely.

Yorke watched the Sergeant till he was swallowed up by the fog, then shut the door and went back into the warm, lit room. He did not return to his correspondence however, but switched off the reading lamp, dropped into his chair by the fire, and stretched his long legs to the blaze. "What Sergeant Tucker wants," he murmured, "is a nice, definite corpse," and he giggled.

He was still smiling when someone passed the window. It was Philipson. As if the sight of his partner reminded Yorke of an anxiety which had for the time been forgotten, he sat up in his chair, pouting his lips and pinching them together with his fingers—a habit of his when he was thinking hard.

6

JUSTINA DISLIKES AN ATMOSPHERE

AFTER DINNER—the Tellwrights had dinner at midday—Justina came into the kitchen to help Martha to wash up, although Tuesday, and not Wednesday, was Martha's afternoon out.

Their conversation, while Justina dried the tumblers, and even most of the silver, was of casual matters, but it was spasmodic, for Martha was wondering why Miss Justina had come to help, and Justina was trying to hit upon a method of approach so gradual, so subtle, that the subject it introduced should melt into its surroundings like Mr. Kipling's leopard among the shadows of a tropical forest. This subject, which Justina had lately found more and more difficult to introduce casually, while the temptation to introduce it had been growing stronger, was Mr. Philipson.

A year ago, when Justina had reversed her original judgment upon Philipson, Martha had been the earliest recipient of the news that "Mr. Philipson's a jolly good sort, really——" and of the anecdote that proved it. But in those days there had been no embarrassment, and no calculation needed in mentioning him.

The incident which had established Philipson in Justina's opinion had taken place at the Benmarsh R.S.P.C.A. dance,

always known to the Tellwrights as "The Animals' Dance."
Justina had attended this function, as always, with enthusiasm; Philipson for the first time, with the utmost unwillingness, and in a vile temper. He would indeed never have
dreamed of going had he not been coerced by Yorke, who
found that he had one young woman too many on his hands,
and that one not very good looking. Justina did not know this,
and she certainly did not guess that the winged words which
changed her opinion of Mr. Philipson were, in strict fact,
merely the expression of his smouldering indignation against
elegant young men who attended dances. The version which
Justina gave to Martha next morning was distinctly more
favorable to him than the truth would have been.

Late up, and breakfasting in homely comfort at the corner
of the kitchen table—Dad was out, and so there was no one
to talk to if she ate in the dining room—Justina gave Martha
an account of the frocks, partners, and incidents of the night
before, while Martha rolled out pastry for mince pies.

"Well then," Justina referred again to her scribbled and
weather-beaten programme—"after the supper dance I had
one with Luke Cane. He's a nice boy, and growing up like
anything. Do you remember when he used to come in here in
shorts and a jersey and ask you for roast potatoes out of the
oven? And now he thinks he's got a moustache. I shouldn't
have known, only he asked me did I like it. Is there any more
coffee?"

There was. Justina got it, and returned to the programme.

"The next was with Mr. Yorke—Miller's Green. You know,
the two men who've started chickens there."

Such family shorthand was sufficient for Martha. She
nodded.

"A beautiful dancer, Martha, like—like cream, you know."
Justina's drawl drew out the word to the utmost extremity of
languorous smoothness. "But I should think," she added
severely, "a bit of a Miss Cissy." In that she had misjudged
him, but the perfunctory remarks which, with a kind of weary
politeness, Mr. Yorke had directed across the top of her head,
were responsible for her error.

Justina, glancing again at the smudged pencil hieroglyphs, giggled.

"Oh, Martha, then—really I couldn't help it—but I'd promised the next to Mr. Heap, and you know he's simply all feet and knees. You just can't keep clear of him. So I faded out to the cloak room and sat by the fire."

She did not ask Martha's verdict upon the ethics of such behaviour, but Martha felt that it was desired, so she gave it.

"I think meself," she said stoutly, "it's downright silly of an old chap like that wanting to dance at all."

"Oh, he's not a bad old thing," Justina remarked, with some compunction. But her mind was full of what had happened as she came from her lurking place at the beginning of the next dance.

"Then—this is what I was going to tell you about that Mr. Philipson, Martha. When I came back, there were some men standing in the doorway; people hadn't begun to dance yet, so I waited a minute for them to move." Justina paused. She was red again to the ears with indignation, almost as red as she had been last night. "And one of them said—he was one of the crowd staying at Marling House—nose like a plug—" Justina snorted. "*He* said—'Just look at the Reverend bloke going round doing the festive. Comic, isn't it?' It was Dad, talking to the band. Well, before I could say anything, or even cough, Mr. Philipson—he was just inside the room—he turned round, absolutely glared, and said in a regular 'damn your eyes' voice—'The Vicar is a friend of mine.' That shut the creature up."

Justina laughed angrily; then she smiled, and the smile was not angry. "I made Dad make Mr. Philipson dance with me after. I don't think that he enjoyed it. He can't dance for toffee. But I wanted to be nice to him. Though I don't think he enjoyed that any better," she concluded with her usual candour. "I should say he was mortally afraid of women."

That was all a year ago, but today to bring Mr. Philipson's name into the conversation seemed to need as much prevision as the move that gives checkmate. She tried to induce Martha to do it, but whether from perversity or lack of penetration, Martha did not oblige, and Justina had to do it for herself.

She managed it from the china closet, while she was putting away the dishes. Anything unnatural in her voice would be explained by the accoustics of the cupboard.

"They didn't eat much of that jam thing last night," she called. The pudding so curtly described was a confection of some subtlety which had taken her a large part of yesterday afternoon to create, but which now she despised, because Philipson had eaten of it with as little interest as if it had been rice pudding.

"Men don't go in much for sweet things generally," Martha comforted her from the sink.

Justina corrected the statement.

"Mr. Philipson's rather a sugar-baby generally." She came back to the kitchen. The boat was launched, and could now proceed under its own steam. "D'you know, Martha, I thought last night he wasn't—he was—well he was sort of queer last night. Did you notice anything?"

"P'raps he'd a chill on his stomach. It's that sort of weather," Martha suggested.

Justina considered the diagnosis, but rejected it.

"He may have had a headache," she said. "He kept feeling his head as if it was sore. Perhaps he's been having a scrap with someone. We'll be having him wanted by the police next!" She laughed. She often laughed at her thoughts of Mr. Philipson, as if they needed something in the nature of salt to disguise their flavour.

"He's a provoking person," she told Martha. "Though I like him," she added, as if it were necessary in the cause of justice.

Martha did not smile.

That afternoon Justina had determined to finish her collecting for the Nursing Association. Most of it she had done, but there was Oldners Farm still to do. So, after lunch, she took her bicycle and started off.

The way there seemed long and mournful in the smothering fog. Justina was glad when she reached it, though the mute face of the house looked sour, dirty and sad. Only in one window, the window of Mrs. Marshall's parlour, was a subdued but warm glow of firelight. "Entertaining friends," Justina thought. "Bother! Hope I shan't have to go in." She rapped smartly and decisively on the door.

For as long as she could count twenty there was no answer, and no sound in the house.

Then, just as she raised her hand to knock again, she heard a slight noise. Someone pushed back a chair, but softly, and as softly a door inside was opened. After that there was silence again. Then suddenly someone called out:

"Who's that?"

Justina was startled. If she had not been so sure of herself she would have been frightened.

"It's all right," she answered. "It's Miss Tellwright."

She heard the bolt shot, the key turned. Then Mrs. Marshall opened the door. At the sight of her Justina thought— "The woman's ill, that is what it is," and stepped quickly inside.

"What's the matter?" she said, and shut the door behind her. It was almost dark in the little passage.

"Nothing's the matter," Mrs. Marshall answered, backing away into the sitting room. "What d'you mean? Nothing's the matter. What d'you want?"

Justina kept her head because she was trained to do that, but she felt very uncomfortable and quite at sea.

"I thought you weren't feeling well. It's all right. What I came for was your Nursing Association sub: One and six———"

Her voice, cool and slow, helped Mrs. Marshall to get hold of herself again.

"Oh yes." She spoke now in quite a normal tone. "Come in, miss."

Justina went in. She sat down on the edge of the horsehair sofa.

"I've never been into this room before," she said conversationally, wondering as she spoke if its musty primness were worse or better than the dismal squalor of the farm kitchen. "How is your husband?"

Mrs. Marshall had shut the door and come back to the hearthrug. She did not answer.

Justina, thinking her question had not been heard, and unable to think of another, began again: "How——?"

"Haven't you heard?" Mrs. Marshall interrupted.

Justina shook her head.

"He's gone."

"Where? What do you mean?"

There was another pause. Then Mrs. Marshall said, deliberately and emphatically: "No one knows."

Justina, used to Benmarsh villagers, expected a flood of tears to follow this. Though she had learnt to deal tolerantly and efficiently with them, she was relieved that this time there were no tears at all. Yet she was puzzled; and stranger still, there was no spate of detail. Her questions elicited the fact that Marshall had been missing since yesterday afternoon; but no further information was forthcoming.

It was Mrs. Marshall who, almost roughly, shelved the subject. "I'll get you the money," she said and, picking up the lamp, went out of the room.

Justina, rather than sit in the dark, followed. Mrs. Marshall crossed the passage, flung open the door of the kitchen opposite, paused for just that half second which a woman will, if she fears mice or cockroaches or some other unpleasantness, and then went in.

Justina, standing just inside the door, wished she had stayed in the other room. The kitchen was chill, yet the air was thick with old, stale smells. "A cold frowst," she thought, with an effort keeping her face expressionless. "Much worse than a warm one."

She watched Mrs. Marshall rummaging in the drawers of the old bureau in the corner. At first, with a professional eye, she noticed only how unsteady the woman's hands were. Then, with an eye not at all professional, she saw something else.

The lamp stood on the table, and it must have been some trick of the light which, welling up from below, showed her Mrs. Marshall's head, face, and throat, as if for the first time. And for the first time, in that soft and strange illumination, she saw the beauty which Philipson had seen. But besides the beauty she saw also that other quality captured by Philipson's picture, a quality to which, at the moment, Justina refused to give a name, though she found it as distasteful to her mind as the stale smell of the room had been to her nose.

Without knowing what she was doing, she moved abruptly to the door. The sudden movement drew from Mrs. Marshall a start and a gasp. She faced Justina across the golden light of the lamp.

Recalled to her duty by the obvious signs of Mrs. Marshall's nervousness, Justina made a violent effort to speak as she would have spoken to any of the other villagers in trouble.

"Look here, Mrs. Marshall. Don't you think we could arrange for someone to sleep up here with you, while you're alone. It must be frightfully lonely when——"

Mrs. Marshall interrupted her. She didn't want anyone, and wouldn't have anyone, and she'd thank everybody if they'd mind their own business. The end of the interview was as uncomfortable, and for Justina, as inexplicable as the beginning. She was immensely relieved when she got on her bicycle again outside the gate.

· At home Justina imparted to the Vicar, and to Martha who was bringing in tea, the news of Marshall's disappearance. But it was no news to them. The Vicar had heard it from a churchwarden; Martha had heard it from the milkman. Mr. Tellwright's opinion was that Marshall would soon turn up again; Martha's that it would be no loss if he didn't. Justina did not express an opinion. She was thinking not of the farmer but of his wife.

That evening after supper her father was allowed a glimpse into her thoughts. For a long time she had sat in silence, knitting quickly and with determination. At last, and suddenly, she lifted her eyes and looked across the hearthrug at him.

"How that man," she began, and paused to pick up a stitch. "How that man managed to sit and paint a portrait in that atmosphere, I don't know."

When Mr. Tellwright inquired as to who, whose, and

which, she told him briefly and scornfully, "Mr. Philipson. Mrs. Marshall. At Oldners Farm."

"Oh!" said the Vicar mildly. "You called there? Was it—thick?"

"Thick?" Justina's nose wrinkled as it had not been allowed to do in the farm kitchen. She tried to refrain from any further comment, failed, and exploded.

"But it's not that so much. It's the woman, Mrs. Marshall. She's a—she's a——" Justina stopped and shut her mouth hard; because you couldn't say a word like that to Dad.

But Mr. Tellwright had comprehended both her self-control, and her meaning. He murmured gently:

"Justina, you've no grounds——"

She shook her head. "We nurses," she told him sternly, "learn to know—things like that."

Mr. Tellwright made no more audible protest. To himself he was saying: "Bless the child! Does she think I haven't?" and his mind dissolved into a sort of tender laughter at her.

But, though at any other time he might have stayed to tease, he did not now. Justina's face, though resolute in expression, had not its usual serenity, and he was pretty sure that he knew where the shoe pinched. He came as near to the point as possible.

"I expect artists get all sorts of people for their models," he said.

Her outburst had relieved Justina's mind. "I suppose so. And I suppose they paint the same model over and over again. Get into a kind of habit of it, don't they?"

The Vicar, keeping to the safe plural of generalities, replied that he believed they did.

7

SEVEN MEN SEARCH FOR A BODY

ABOUT THREE O'CLOCK in the afternoon, but in such an unnatural twilight that one of its members had put a flash lamp into his pocket, the search party, headed by Sergeant Tucker, arrived at Miller's Green. Yorke heard the shuffle of its feet in the hall; then Mrs. Harker announced it.

"And shall I tell Mr. Philipson, sir? The Sergeant asked for him as well as for you." Mrs. Harker's sniff seemed to imply that she thought Sergeant Tucker's a strange taste.

Yorke got up slowly.

"Take 'em into the kitchen," he said. "Mr. Philipson has gone out, you can tell the Sergeant. I'll be ready in a minute."

It was rather more than five minutes before Yorke came down again in a Burberry, thick boots and leggings. Whatever he was going to do, he dressed suitably. The search party was closeted with Mrs. Harker in the kitchen, but though the kitchen door stood ajar, no murmur of conversation came from inside. When Yorke pushed the door open it became obvious that Mrs. Harker was not one of those cooks who have an irresistible *penchant* for policemen. Sergeant Tucker sat, nursing his helmet, on one of a row of wooden chairs; upon the others perched, as tentatively, the rest of the search party.

Mrs. Harker occupied the only comfortable chair in the
kitchen, but it was wasted on her. Bolt upright, with feet
firmly planted on the rag rug she sat, looking down her nose
at some chilly white crochet that jerked and waggled limply
in her quick fingers.

The alacrity with which Mrs. Harker's guests rose to their
feet was a tribute, which she did not fail to appreciate, to her
force of character. Yet, as they trooped out after the Sergeant,
they were uncomfortably conscious of the spoor, as of herding
elephants, which they left upon the red and blue tiles of the
kitchen floor. Even the chilly and dismal world outside
seemed hospitable, compared with the frigidity of the atmosphere which surrounded Mrs. Harker.

The relief which one and all experienced was however
mitigated by the fact that the party was not, like the city which
is blessed, at unity with itself. Besides Yorke the Sergeant's
helpers consisted of Jakes from the ferry, Mansell the sexton,
Halliwell from the general shop, Marsh of the Blue Boar—
and Peppard.

Sergeant Tucker had certainly not invited Peppard to
come; it was sheer bad luck for him that the garage proprietor
had heard in time of the work that was afoot. Mansell it was,
a stranger to the district, and ignorant of the Peppard-Tucker
feud, who had passed on what he felt sure would be a succulent item of news; not every day in Benmarsh were Pilly's
Ponds dragged for corpses, And certaily Peppard was interested, and to Mansell's way of thinking, most helpful. At once
he charged his informant with a message to the Sergeant; he
would himself help in the dragging of the Ponds, and would
bring a car round to the Sergeant's house to pick up the party
at two-thirty sharp. Mansell's assignation was for three o'clock
but Peppard was not going to allow Sergeant Tucker to get
off without him.

So now Peppard climbed into the driver's seat of the roomy,
tall old taxi he had brought, and Mansell got up beside him.
Sergeant Tucker and the other three fitted themselves in
behind, giving Yorke as much room as they possibly could;
they were a mass of inferiority complexes after their treatment
by Mrs. Harker.

There was little conversation as the car trundled through the lanes; at their feet, a reminder, if it had been needed, that this was no pleasure party, lay an iron grapnel, some bricks and a coil of rope. The grapnel was a familiar object to all of them; its ordinary occupation was to retrieve lost buckets from cottagers' wells. But today it had become a thing of sinister import; it was not a bucket that the curved iron fingers would be groping for, in the underwater darkness and slime.

Pilly's Ponds, a chain of three small pools connected by a small stream, were pleasant places in summer—the resort of many picnickers, and of those dumb and awkward couples which are the lover and his lass of cold reality. But now, as the car drew up on the grass verge of the road, and the search party issued from all its doors at once, none of them thought of Pilly's Ponds with any sentiment of pleasure.

The pools lay close, at the bottom of a short but steep slope; yet so thick was the fog that nothing could be seen of them. Only the tops of the nearer birch trees, which in summer made such a grateful light shade down the hillside and upon the water, swam uncertainly out of the chill vapour. Everything else in the world but these, a patch of road, the wall, and a stretch of hillside, was blotted out, as if it had fallen away or melted into nothing, and only the ground under their feet was solid. The quiet too, especially after the hoarse mechanical rumble of the car, startled their ears. While they stamped their feet on the road and straightened their coats, they spoke only in low voices; when they were silent the silence was complete; there was no sound anywhere; not a bird, not an animal seemed left alive.

They followed Sergeant Tucker over the stile, and down the slippery path. Peppard came last, and a little way behind the others, as though in some measure at least he was determined to disassociate himself from them. But Yorke turned back and waited for him.

"Well, Peppard," he said, and his voice, as that of everyone else, was subdued, "what do *you* think of this business?"

Peppard did not seem to appreciate Yorke's affability. He

mumbled something indistinctly, and then, "Damn this path! It wants a nice bit of gravel on it, it's that slippery."

But Yorke was not to be put off.

"Have you any theory?" he asked. "We're all detectives," he added lightly, "when it comes to a case near home."

"What do you think?" Peppard countered defensively.

"Oh, I've not been long enough in Benmarsh to know— well—what would be likely to happen to Marshall."

He and Peppard had reached the foot of the slope and now stood a little apart from the others; Peppard seemed to wish to join them, even though Sergeant Tucker, busy with the grapnel and rope, was the centre of interest; but Yorke stood in the way, feet apart and hands on his hips.

"Of course," said Yorke persuasively, "there are quite a lot of things it could be. He may have gone off on purpose, or been injured—or killed—on the road, or fallen in here in the dark as the Sergeant seems to think—or even committed suicide."

Peppard's face expressed extreme and uncomfortable indecision.

"There is something else too," he growled at last.

"Oh? What?" Yorke looked expectant, a little alarmed.

"Murder," Peppard muttered, and looked as if he were ashamed of having mentioned it, and fidgeted awkwardly with his feet. He seemed unwilling to meet Mr. Yorke's eye.

"Have you——" Yorke began, and cleared his throat. "Have you any grounds for thinking it is—that?"

Peppard looked up now at Yorke's face. But Yorke was staring at the surface of the pool as it lay, dull and sullen under the lightless atmosphere. Peppard glanced away again.

"Well——" he began and stopped.

"Did you go up to Oldners Farm that day?" Yorke asked. "Or did you see anything that——?"

"No. I didn't go there." Peppard affirmed energetically. He hesitated, then added: "I was up the road towards Ipsden." But Yorke ignored this bit of information.

"I don't think," said he, "that murder is very likely. A getaway or an accident is much nearer the mark, *I* should say."

Peppard murmured something indistinctly. He wanted very much to terminate the conversation, but as a born controversialist he found it hard to simulate agreement. A dull splash interrupted them; Sergeant Tucker had fixed the grapnel, and thrown it in; the business was about to begin; Peppard took his opportunity, skirted Yorke's jutting elbow, and joined the rest of the party.

"Will you take one end of the line, sir?" Tucker spoke to Yorke, who nodded in silence, took the rope, and following Tucker's directions, went off along the banks of the pond till the others lost sight of him in the mist. Only the line which led from Tucker's hand into the sullen water above the grapnel, and out again into invisibility, connected him with them. The farther part jerked and moved as Mr. Yorke moved. tightening now and again, and then flopping back into the water with a small sighing splash. After a few minutes Yorke's voice came out of the mist——

"Right, Sergeant."

"Move on then!"

In silence the men moved forward, their minds following the grapnel as it nosed its bland way along the muddy bottom of the pool, feeling for a dead man. Once Mansell, a nervous subject, let out a cry——

"Look there! A face!"

They looked, none of them quite unshaken. But the white blur was only a bit of old newspaper.

Sergeant Tucker was nothing if not thorough. By the time he was satisfied that Pilly's Ponds did not contain any dead body, most members of the search party were sick and tired of them. Yorke was not one of these, but when some spirits were ready to fail, he it was who lent his voice to the Sergeant for "making a thorough, good job of it." Peppard too was staunch. When Mansell muttered to him that it was all rot, and quite time to give over, Peppard, for once, vindicated the Sergeant.

"But you mark my words," he told Mansell, "if it's not here, it's somewhere else. And it may be put here yet. Tucker thinks that now we've dragged the Ponds we'll be sure it isn't here. But if the murderer has any sense it's just where he'll put it."

Yorke overheard the last words, and turned quickly.

"Good gracious, Peppard, how ingenious! Lucky for the murderer—if there is one—that you're not a policeman."

Peppard said no more till Yorke had moved away. He did not enjoy being laughed at. But he put his mouth close to Marshall's ear: "When it *is* found, someone I saw along the Ipsden road yesterday will be sorry for it."

Mansell, as intended, asked: "Who?"

"Never you mind," Peppard rebuked him. "I'll tell Tucker if he asks me, and perhaps if he doesn't. But I'll tell you this. He had blood all over his hands."

"Oo!" said Mansell.

So well occupied had the party been by the Sergeant that it was only when at last they climbed up again to the car, that they realized that the fog had for some time been thinning, a white light had succeeded the sulky lowering gloom, and the impalpable walls had withdrawn, leaving visible trees, hillside, and below them the dark pools. By the time Peppard deposited Yorke, the last of the party, at Miller's Green, there was no fog at all, and to the west the brownish clouds were puddled with the faintest touch of chill gold.

Yorke dined alone again that night. Philipson, who had been to his dentist, came home with a scarf wound round the lower part of his face, and told Mrs. Harker, in a muffled voice, that he only wanted soup, and that he would have it in bed. Mrs. Harker herself carried it up to him, her own weariness, so she made clear to Agnes, ignored in the cause of propriety. With no more ambiguity, though in silence, she gave Mr. Philipson to understand that to want soup in bed when dinner had to be served downstairs, was unworthy of a gentleman. The ancient gods must have experienced much the same discomfort at the grudging offerings of coerced Christians, as the unfortunate Mr. Philipson when he took the tray from Mrs. Harker's hands.

It was not till breakfast next morning that Yorke and Philipson met; the fog had come down again, and if anything thicker than ever, but Yorke's mood was almost aggressively cheerful. In the bathroom he had been intermittently tuneful, and he was still singing softly to himself when he broke into the dining room. Philipson was tentatively eating an egg, with an anxious expression, and his head slightly on one side. He looked unusually small, shabby and fretful, and when Yorke inquired "had he heard the news" he answered with nothing more encouraging than a mumble.

"Well," said Yorke cheerfully, "old Marshall has been and gone and disappeared."

Yorke was pouring out his coffee at the hot plate, but he turned as he spoke and looked sidelong at his partner whose back was towards him. Philipson sat still for a few seconds, his spoon suspended in the air over his egg. Then he dug it in again and went on eating.

"Oh!" was all he said.

Yorke came back to the table.

"Tucker and search party, self included, dragged all three of Pilly's Ponds yesterday afternoon. Total bag—a very dead dog, bits of an umbrella, and an old perambulator. Oh yes—and some boots—presentation boots to tramps I expect."

Philipson pushed away his egg, and rather pointedly took up the *Daily Mirror*.

"But I assure you," said Yorke, "Benmarsh could hardly have been more interested if we'd fished up a string of corpses." Philipson rattled the pages, but Yorke went on, merely raising his voice a little. "I took the car that way last night, and I can tell you 'Round the Marble Arch' wasn't in it. All the girls and their boys were there looking at the place where a corpse hadn't been found."

Philipson spread the paper wide; only the rough grey bush of his hair showed above it. He had been listening after all, for now he asked——

"But what—has happened to old Marshall?"

"You can search me," said Yorke.

After a minute Philipson inquired: "When did he disappear?"

"Last seen—no—supposed to have been in Mallingford between five and seven-thirty last night. It was that letter that came for me this morning—(d'you remember? I told you about it)—that gave Sergeant Tucker that clue."

·"Oh well," said Philipson, "I suppose he'll turn up somewhere."

Mrs. Harker, always alive to Mr. Yorke's moods, was not likely to overlook his unusual gaiety on this very unpromising morning. He was still in the dining room, lighting his pipe, when she came in to clear away breakfast.

"And how do you like this weather, Mrs. Harker?" he inquired when he had waved his hand to the littered table, and adjured her to "Carry on."

Mrs. Harker didn't.

"Foul, isn't it?" Mr. Yorke agreed. "And I'm going out after dinner this evening—right over to Tetcot."

The prospect did not seem to daunt him,.for he lounged out of the dining room, humming, and left Mrs. Harker convinced that what he was going to Tetcot tonight for, was to propose to one of the Miss Veres. "He's that lively and excited," she said to herself. "I hope she's a nice young lady." Mrs. Harker lost herself in daydreams of a reorganized household, with no Mr. Philipson and a very ladylike and incompetent Mrs. Yorke. A Frigidaire occupied an important place in the dream, for the larder at Miller's Green was inclined to be damp, and was a perpetual subject of lamentation with Mrs. Harker.

Her theory as to Mr. Yorke's intentions was expounded that morning during the relaxation of "elevenses," to an audience of Miss Smith, who came to mend once a week, and Agnes—after this committee or two thirds of it had examined and debated the disappearance of old Marshall. Agnes herself would not have been favoured with Mrs. Harker's forecast of Mr. Yorke's future, but Miss Smith was of an age, respectability, and standing that made her a person to whom

Mrs. Harker might impart her news. For by that time, and under the beneficent influence of hot cocoa with plenty of cream in it, the thing was news—or almost news, with only the qualifying "You mark my words" to differentiate it from historic fact.

"No," she recapitulated, more for her own sake than for her hearers, "he didn't exactly say so, but I could tell there was something up by the way he spoke. He was sort of . . ." Mrs. Harker fixed her eyes on the butcher's calendar, a highly coloured garden scene, and strove for words to describe Mr. Yorke's condition. "He was strung up like," she said, a little doubtfully, as if feeling that this did not quite do the subject justice. "Uplifted as the saying is. And when he said to me: 'I'm going out in the car tonight, Mrs. Harker,' I knew what he meant as if he'd told me. He had to clear his throat like as he'd a frog in it, and he sounded sort of shy and queer like . . . as if he were meaning something more than he said."

Miss Smith—after all she was a spinster, and had not heard the significant intonation of Mr. Yorke's voice—put in a demurrer. She did not think, she said, that Mr. Yorke looked like a marrying man. Proper bachelor he looked, she said—looked as if he looked after himself as well as a cat. Now the other gentleman, she opined, needed someone to do things for him.

Agnes broke into the conversation with a gulp of nervousness.

"Yes and I saw him—Mr. Philipson I mean—yesterday afternoon talking to Miss Tellwright at the end of Oldners Lane. 'E did look sweet on her too, and no mistake. I says to myself, 'There's something up there.' "

But Mrs. Harker, nettled by Miss Smith's reception of her news, turned, with all the more savage joy, upon this scapegoat which had delivered itself into her hand. While Agnes was being reduced to a crimson-faced silence, Miss Smith sipped her cocoa and looked disapproval at all gossip, idleness and tattling; yet in this she was not playing fair, for while by her silence she lent her tacit support to Mrs. Harker, she was planning to go round by the Vicarage to see if she could worm out of Martha Haworth, the Vicar's cook-housekeeper, any confirmation of Agnes' surmise.

Miss Smith went, but she learnt nothing from Martha. After an oblique approach by way of a comment on "the Vicar's beautiful sermon" and the dearth of marriages—"only one 'for the third time of asking' last Sunday"—Miss Smith came into the open with——

"But what's this I hear about Miss Justina?"

Martha looked at her. "Well, what is it?"

"About her and Mr. Philipson."

"What about 'em?"

Miss Smith was driven to an embarrassed giggle.

"I heard it was a case between them."

Martha looked straight at her again.

"First any one's told me about it," she said.

Miss Smith had to own herself defeated.

8

PHILIPSON NEEDS A
SLEEPING DRAUGHT

AT HALF-PAST FIVE that same Thursday afternoon
Justina Tellwright leapt from her bicycle, shoved
it against the wall, and bounded up the two steps of the village
post office, with just half a split second to catch the mail. But
at the door she had to stop, for a man was coming out; in fact,
as she charged in, head down, she almost butted him in the
chest. She stopped dead, and so did he. It was Philipson.

"Oh," said Justina, very red, "I'm sorry."

Philipson said nothing; he only gave a sort of choked gasp
as he stepped back.

"Wait for me," said Justina over her shoulder, "I've got a
message for you."

Her voice was cheerful; her mind, as she bought her stamps,
was not. She had seen, what perhaps any but a trained nurse
would have missed, the twitch and whitening of Philipson's
face when he started back. As she licked the stamps, laid them
on the envelopes and thumped them smartly into place,
Philipson passed, temporarily perhaps, perhaps too only super-
ficially, from the category of friends to that of cases. But he
was a case in which she was passionately interested.

She found him outside, waiting obediently but cheerlessly in the chill fog. She had time to notice that his chin was not even yet quite steady. He looked up and saw her, and she took her eyes quickly from his face.

"Which way are you going?" she asked.

"Why?"

As firmly and candidly as if she and Philipson had gone back to the easy terms of a week—of two days ago, she answered:

"Because I'll come a little way with you." But the firmness and candour were of the nurse; to the nurse it does not matter that a patient would gladly be rid of her company.

It was evident that Philipson was trying to think of some alternative plan; he failed. While she got her bicycle he stood with shoulders hunched, then turned in the direction of Miller's Green. She fell into step beside him.

"Dad told me to ask you if you'd go and play chess with him tomorrow night. I was just coming to Miller's Green, but now I needn't."

Philipson's relief was tacit, but none the less apparent.

"Yes," he said hastily. "All right. I will. Thank you."

"Good!" said Justina cheerfully. If Philipson had known her in the hospital he would have recognized the bracing, hygienic tone.

"Dad will be alone," she went on, "I'm off to a new case tomorrow—got a wire last night. It may last a week or a fortnight or months." But how, she was asking herself, can I find out what's wrong with him?

They came to the turning by the A.A. Box. The main road, or the small space of it they could see between the walls of mist, was deserted.

"Beastly day," said Philipson, "I shouldn't come any farther if I were you."

"No, I won't." Justina wheeled her bicycle round, then spoke:

"Look here, Mr. Philipson, I may be butting in, but—are you sleeping badly?"

He gave her a look that she was unwilling to think was suspicious, and hesitated a minute. Then:

"Yes—rather," he answered cautiously.

"Have you tried anything for it?"

"No—I'm all right. It'll be all right," he affirmed. His voice sounded irritable but his appearance was dejected, and Justina was used to irritable patients.

She bent over her bicycle bell, as though its mechanism suddenly interested her, and she made it ping-ping gently.

"If I were you," she said, "I wouldn't let it go on without taking something. Insomnia's much harder to cure if it gets to be a habit. Try a hot bath and a hot whiskey and some aspirin." She stuck out her hand. "Good-bye."

Philipson took it stiffly, and as stiffly said: "Good-bye."

He had not told Justina that he would follow her medical advice, and indeed he had not the slightest intention of following it. With the perversity of Naaman the Syrian he was annoyed with her for suggesting such a simple, commonplace nostrum as a palliative for the immense evil that overshadowed him. It was not till close on dinner time that he suddenly changed his mind about that, and about Justina. All day he had been telling himself fiercely, angrily, and miserably, that he must have nothing to do with Justina Tellwright—that he must not even think of her. But now, as he sat with his head on his hands alone in the sitting room, he forgot for a moment to be fierce and angry, and felt only miserable. Such a softening, and the gush of self pity that went with it, altered his attitude towards aspirin and whiskey. He felt suddenly that he must take them. Justina had wanted him to take them, and besides, he could not face another night like the last trying the only thing he knew of which might save him.

Once he had decided he was eaten up with impatience to be doing what Justina had advised. Mrs. Harker, very busy and heated in the kitchen, was both surprised and annoyed to see Mr. Philipson's untidy head pushed round the door, and to be asked to keep up a good fire because he wanted a hot bath, a really hot bath, and was there plenty of whiskey, because he would be wanting a hot drink too?

Mrs. Harker, electing to suppose that Mr. Philipson intended not only a reflection on her management of the furnace, but an accusation of tampering with the whiskey supply, told him a variety of things about hot water, furnaces, and her own teetotal principles. But Mr. Philipson, with an asperity and decision unusual in him, and therefore startling, interrupted the flow of her indignation.

"Well, see that the water's hot anyway. Really hot, you understand." He shut the door smartly upon whatever reply there might have been.

The next thing he must do was to make sure that he had some aspirin. He was certain there was a bottle in his collar drawer, at least half full. But, when he came to hunt for it, no bottle could he find except an ancient one with the label half scratched off, and half a broken tablet inside which might well, he thought, not be aspirin at all, but a throat gargle. This was awful. He dug into the always perturbed contents of his chest of drawers like a terrier in a flower bed. The result was that he found a quantity of articles long lost, but he did not find any aspirin.

Yorke, wallowing luxuriously in a stinging hot bath, with the hot tap still turned on, and the water dribbling out of the waste, heard a heavy knock at the door.

"I say, Yorke!" came Philipson's voice, and the door handle was rattled violently.

Yorke surged up out of the water, and turned off the tap. "What is it?" he cried, resentful, as any man might be who has legitimately bagged the bathroom.

"Have you got any aspirins?"

"No."

"Oh! damn!"

Philipson's footsteps receded. Yorke turned the tap on again and flopped back. Above the rush and gurgle of water he heard Philipson call out from the top of the stairs. He thought he said: "Don't be long."

"All right!" he shouted savagely. But he had no intention

of being hurried, and resumed the idle pleasure of splashing and dabbling in the water with his hands. As he lay there he remembered that he had actually bought some aspirin a few weeks ago. He would take them down to dinner with him. Philipson could wait for them, as he must wait for the bathroom.

But when Yorke came down into the sitting room, jingling in his hand the little bottle of pills, Philipson was not there. Yorke waited a few minutes, then went into the dining room. He liked his dinner hot, and had no intention of letting it spoil for Philipson's sake. He did not hurry over his fish, but when he had finished the course there was still no Philipson. When he got up to ring the bell for Mrs. Harker he went out into the hall and shouted upstairs: "Philipson! Philipson!"

The unlighted landing above was silent. He ran up a few steps and saw that Philipson's door stood ajar. There was no light in the room.

Mrs. Harker, coming in with an expression of veiled triumph and a perfect pigeon pie, saw at once that something had gone wrong.

"Where's Mr. Philipson?" Yorke threw at her.

"Am I your partner's keeper?" was the gist of her reply.

"Has he gone out?" said Yorke.

Mrs. Harker admitted to having heard the front door bang.

"Did he go to the garage?"

Mrs. Harker, her feelings seared by Mr. Yorke's fierce tone, mumbled that she couldn't say for certain, sir.

Yorke half rose from his chair. Then he sat down again.

"Oh, I know," he said as if to himself. "He's only gone for some aspirin." To Mrs. Harker he said that Mr. Philipson wouldn't be long.

But he was long. The garage had been searched and found empty and Yorke had been standing by the sitting-room fire, keeping his shins and his anger warm for nearly half an hour when a car drew up at the gate. But Yorke knew that it was not his car. Then who——? He listened, frowning. Could something have happened?

The garden gate gave its musical whine as it opened. Someone was coming up the path. There sounded the unmistakable scrape and click of a latchkey, inserted and turned. So it was Philipson. Yorke heard him go up the hall to the coat pegs, then there was silence for a moment—yet not silence, for in the road the engine of a car still gently throbbed.

When the sitting-room door opened Philipson was there, looking acutely embarrassed and apprehensive.

Yorke said, in a voice that would have startled his partner if he had not already been so flurried:

"Where's my car?"

Philipson went across the room with something of the sidelong hurried and unobtrusive gait of a crab. He laid a little white packet on his desk.

"I really am most awfully sorry, Yorke. I—I'm afraid I butted her into a wall in the fog. It was on the way home, just by Peppard's. I really was being careful, but the fog's terribly thick. I really am frightfully sorry. It's only the steering Peppard says, and he'll have her tracked and ready tomorrow."

"Tomorrow!" said Yorke and stopped to get better control of his voice. "How dare you take my car like that!"

This time Philipson was startled, so startled that instinctively he stepped back from the furious young man who had borne down upon him.

"I tell you I'm sorry——" he protested again, and then remembered what Yorke's anger had made him forget. "But you told me I could take it. I asked you."

Yorke, at Philipson's movement, had pulled himself up. He turned about now and went back to the fire.

"When did I?" he asked. Not that it really mattered.

"When you were in the bathroom."

"I——"

"Yes, you did," Philipson cut in. "I said 'Can I take the car? I shan't be long,' and you shouted out 'All right.' "

Yorke remembered now. He muttered, but to himself: "And I had the blasted things all the time."

"I'm really most awfully sorry," Philipson repeated his parrotlike, useless apology.

Yorke swung round, and went over to the phone.

"Oh, shut up!" he cried furiously. "What is Peppard's number?"

Philipson interrupted eagerly.

"Wait a minute. That's all fixed up. I was just going to tell you. I've got Peppard outside—I asked him to lend us a car but he couldn't tonight. But he'll take you over and call for you whenever you like to ring him up. It's my pigeon of course."

Yorke had laid his hand upon the phone. He did not take it away for a minute but stood looking down at it in silence. Then he raised his head.

"You blasted ass!" he shouted at Philipson, "I'm not going out in one of Peppard's old rattletraps." He stopped and bit his lip. "Oh, I dare say you couldn't help it, but I never knew such a fool with a car," he added with controlled bitterness.

An uncomfortable and lengthy silence fell. Philipson stood by his desk, fidgeting with the little white packet that had caused all the trouble.

"What about——" he began. "What shall I do about Peppard? Shall I send him away?"

Yorke did not answer for a minute. Then:

"Tell him to go to hell."

Philipson left the room to deliver a modified version of Yorke's orders. When he came back he did not rejoin Yorke, but went instead into the dining room, where after some delay Mrs. Harker provided him with some ruinous remains of dinner. As he made a hasty meal he was unhappily conscious that this row with Yorke had shaken him up pretty badly, started his head aching again, and made still more problematical the quiet sleep for which he longed. But, thought Philipson, how thoroughly spoiled the fellow must be, to fly off the handle like that, and then sulk and refuse to go in a taxi. Wouldn't be seen in it by one of his posh friends, Philipson supposed, and felt scornful of Yorke's snobbery. "Spoiled young puppy he is!" Philipson said to himself, and then remembered that it was better to be a spoiled young puppy than some other things a man could be.

9

THE VICAR RECEIVES A SHOCK

JUSTINA WAS VERY cheerful at supper that night; so was Mr. Tellwright; but only Justina made the mistake of supposing that her counterfeit was taken for the real thing. She, however, went up to bed proud and pleased that she had managed not to spoil, for Dad, her last evening at home.

Breakfast next morning was a different matter. Morning was obviously the time for getting things off your chest, she thought, and besides, it was now or never, because her train left at eleven o'clock. Mr. Tellwright noticed her absent-mindedness during the meal, but said nothing. He spread out *The Times* and hid himself behind it; he guessed, that were he ever so little concealed, Justina would come out into the open; in his dealings with his daughter the Vicar had many of the methods and all the patience of a bird watcher.

Justina picked up a spare table fork, and began digging it into the tablecloth. She continued this occupation for some time in silence. Then she blurted out:

"Dad—I—I heard a horrid thing yesterday." She gave a little angry laugh.

Mr. Tellwright folded and laid down *The Times* but he

kept his eyes on it. Justina should understand, and did, that he was attending, but that he would not look at her.

"I met Mrs. Peppard," she began again, and again stuck.

"I owe Peppard for the taxi last week," the Vicar murmured, and reassured by that delicate pretence of indifference Justina managed to tumble it all out—the horrid, mad, absurd thing that Mrs. Peppard was saying, "but in strict confidence, and only to you, miss," about Mr. Philipson.

"But it's mad, it's crazy, it can't be true, can it, Dad?" she kept on repeating as she told him.

Mr. Tellwright laid his thin hand on *The Times* and held it down as though it were something lively that needed firm treatment.

"You say that Mrs. Peppard, on Peppard's authority, is putting it about that Philipson has"—Mr. Tellwright found that he balked at the word, but there was no other—"that Philipson has murdered old Marshall?"

Justina did not speak. She nodded.

"But——Good Gracious!" said the Vicar.

"Peppard," Justina added, "has told Sergeant Tucker. Mrs. Peppard 'felt that we ought to know.' "

"But," the Vicar began and Justina looked at him, suddenly hopeful. "But after all, why should Philipson—do anything like that? I know he dislikes Marshall, but that is not enough."

Justina prayed inwardly that Dad should not look at her and see her growing red, miserably, shamefully red.

"That's the horridest part," she said hurriedly, and in a hard voice. "They're saying that it's because he—and Mrs. Marshall——"

"I see." The Vicar hastened to interrupt her sentence. "But was he—did he—is he known to have gone to the farm a lot?" he added after a pause.

"He painted her portrait." Justina reminded him.

Mr. Tellwright left that side of the question. Enough had been said. "I don't understand," he objected, "why Peppard thinks that it's murder, and why, if it is, Philipson should have had anything to do with it."

Justina was relieved to get back to this comparatively safe ground. She answered in quite a businesslike tone: "Because he saw Mr. Philipson in the woods on the Ipsden road—'sulking,' Mrs. Peppard said." She stopped, and again succeeded in eliminating all feeling from her voice. "He looked queer and wild, Mrs. Peppard said, and he jumped back into the wood when Peppard came by in the car." Her voice dropped. "Peppard said he had blood on his hands," she said in a whisper.

The Vicar frowned over that, then his face brightened.

"Perhaps he'd cut himself," he suggested stubbornly. "And that's no proof that he'd had anything to do with Marshall's disappearance, unless Marshall is known to have been up the Ipsden road. How does Peppard know that Philipson ever went near Marshall's farm?"

"He doesn't," Justina said.

"Well then——"

"But I do."

Mr. Tellwright was so startled that he looked at her, and then hastily away again.

"At least, I know," said Justina, "that he started off to go there. I met him at the end of the Green Lane on Tuesday; that was when I asked him to come in to supper. He was going up to Marshall's about some honey. I saw him start off up the lane."

Mr. Tellwright, the private, innermost Mr. Tellwright turned, quickly, urgently, confidently, whither he was used to turn in troubles. Then he came back to the breakfast room and Justina.

"Justina," he said. "If it is true—people can do strange things you know—things quite different from what their real self intends—if it is true——"

"Yes?"

"Philipson needs all our kindness—of thought if we can give him nothing else."

Justina got up hastily. She stood behind the Vicar's chair, and with her back to him.

"It's—beastly," she said after a moment. "I—are we beasts?"

"We are," Mr. Tellwright acknowledged serenely.

"You mean we're something else too?"

The Vicar nodded. Justina was not looking at him, but her words were not really a question.

"If you can get that into your head, Justina, you'll never be"—he hesitated for a word—"dismayed. Nor too impatient with the beast."

Justina did not speak for some time, and neither of them moved. After a determined, and for long a doubtful struggle, she was at last victorious. She knew that she would not need to get out her handkerchief. She put up her chin, and moved towards the door.

"Right-o, Dad," she said, and went out of the room. But she did not shut the door, nor did she hurry upstairs.

Nothing more of the matter was said until she was settled in the red-plush third-class railway carriage that smelt of dust, smoke, tobacco, and for Justina, even now, of holidays. Mr. Tellwright, his hat in his hand, stood on the platform. There was no one else in the compartment. Justina said:

"I'll let you have a post card as soon as I get there." And then, as if it were part of the same subject. "I think you ought to tell him, Dad."

Mr. Tellwright did not ask "Whom?" He only said: "All right, Maria."

That was one of her old play-names, and not often used now. They smiled at each other. Justina had reason to be proud of the smile.

Thursday was Mrs. Harker's day out. At two o'clock, clad all in black, except for some widowly mauve flowers in her hat, with a shiny black purse in one hand and, wet or fine, under the other arm an umbrella topped by the torso of a brightly coloured parrot, she pattered out of the gate, and down the lane to catch the Farley bus by the A.A. box. For the rest of the day Agnes was responsible for heating up a series of dishes which Mrs. Harker had already prepared, and concerning which she had dinned into the girl's ears the most minute instructions. Agnes had not an inordinate opinion of her own ability, but she did think she would have managed all right for the gentlemen for once without all that. But she did not dare to say so.

Yorke was out that tea-time, so Agnes, when she brought the tray into the sitting room, counted on a few moments' converse with his partner. In the kitchen Agnes was a staunch, though silent partisan of Mr. Philipson; almost inevitably so, since Mrs. Harker was so strong an advocate for Mr. Yorke. But besides this negative reason for Agnes's preference, "the girl" considered that there was another bond between them. Once, when dusting Mr. Philipson's perpetually tousled papers, she had come on some rough yet lively sketches of a female figure pegging out clothes on a line. That might have been, in itself, inconclusive, for there was not the least attempt at any facial likeness. But in one of the sketches there were unmistakable dots upon the dress. Agnes was not likely to forget that dress. It had been a flag of mutiny, but it had had to be hauled down. For one week, however, maugre Mrs. Harker, Agnes had worn it, and during that week—it was some time during last spring—Mr. Philipson had been sitting in the orchard and she had been hanging out the clothes.

What such a drawing indicated if not the beginning of a love story in the most perfectly romantical style of *Home Chat*, Agnes did not know. For several weeks she went about keyed up to a high pitch of excitement and expectation. Nothing further happened. Mr. Philipson did not seize and press her hand as he passed her on the stairs, nor did she once find waiting for her at home a sheaf of gorgeous hothouse blooms, a gift from the bashfully anonymous admirer. In time the expectation, and the embarrassment, which had been equally acute, died down, yet to Agnes the knowledge of those sketches constituted a tie. She felt that she and Mr. Philipson had an affinity for each other.

Today when she started off from the kitchen with the tea tray, she was wrought up to a high pitch of excitement. For in a moment she was to take the stage in a drama whose title might have been "The Only One Who Trusted Him," and the conversation with Mr. Philipson which was about to open would reach some such climax as:

"I am innocent, Agnes. But no one will believe it."

"*I* believe it."

"You—believe—it! God bless you!" (Curtain).

When she opened the sitting room door, however, the familiar sight of Mr. Philipson seated at his desk, his reading spectacles half way down his nose, withered, with its humdrum familiarity, the fine flower of her opening speech. Instead of what she intended, she told him that the scones were very hot, and mind the lid because it had been in the oven.

Then, screwing up her courage she asked had he heard.

To that conundrum Mr. Philipson replied, without the slightest trace of interest: "No." He did not turn his head; he did not even raise his eyes to look at her.

"It's what," Agnes began, all of a dither, "it's what they're saying in the village. About what happened on Tuesday."

"Tuesday?" Mr. Philipson repeated vaguely; and then, but not vaguely: "Damn the village!" He slammed shut the lid of his desk. "Damn' lot of gossip—Pack of lies, I expect. No. And I don't want to hear it."

He stalked across the room to the tea table and dropped into a chair. Agnes for a moment stood regarding the back of his head, her mouth slightly open. Then she withdrew, in considerable distress of mind, to a solitary, heavily buttered and jammed tea in the kitchen, which comforted her a little.

Many links in the chain of causation—it is a trite reflection —are absurdly weak. Philipson had promised Justina Tellwright to go to the Vicarage that night, but at the time that Agnes brought in his tea he had no intention at all of doing so. He was determined to ring up, apologize, and say that toothache—which seemed to him a less culpable disease than a splitting headache—would prevent him. Then he would go early to bed and sleep—or hope to sleep.

But, as he ate the hot scones, the prospect of dinner served by an Agnes primed with Benmarsh gossip, assumed the proportions and complexion of a nightmare. Rather than that he would keep his promise. And therefore—but he had not the least idea of all the "therefores" which would follow.

The Vicar's study was a snug place for a cold evening, and a room after a man's heart. The chairs, except that which Justina had in her childhood always called "Daddy's Sermon Chair," were all large, and of a comfortable, confidential shabbiness; their old crimson leather had darkened to a shade of purplish red that always pleased Philipson's eye. Their texture pleased him too, and even the damage wrought upon their arms by dynasties of Vicarage cats did not detract from their pleasant aspect, for the little thin triangles of torn leather that freaked them were like the sharp ears of tiny animals with a downy soft undersurface pleasant to finger. The walls of the small room were covered with an accumulation of photographs which would have been a good foundation for a biography of the Vicar, had any one dreamed of writing it. There were yellowing, foggy portraits of himself and his brothers, all with such brilliant eyes that Justina diagnosed congenital thyroid. There were daguerreotypes of an earlier generation of Tellwrights, among them a little girl in a full skirt flounced with velvet and a pair of long, lace-edged, and perfectly tubular drawers beneath. She stood beside a lady who, even in her preposterous costume, alternately puffed and constricted, managed to be both pretty and yet like Justina. Next to the young mother and daughter of those dead years were the Vicar's college groups; over them all and just under the ceiling lay an oar of the Vicar's college eight. Sandwiched in between the portraits were pictures of Italy, of Switzerland, a sketch of an old house—the early Victorian Tellwright had been born there. Beside the fireplace hung a black revolving star chart, a kettle holder, a toasting fork, a case for pipe lighters, a calendar, and a matchbox holder, which, since Justina had only just departed, did contain a matchbox.

Mr. Tellwright pulled himself up out of one of the deep chairs and welcomed Philipson. He said no more than the usual things, but Philipson always felt, because the Vicar's voice was so warm and gentle, and his thin face so full of shining sincerity, that in the Vicarage he had cast anchor for a few hours in a port of peace.

Tonight, however, it was not so, for he had brought his cargo of care with him. The one comfort was that with the Vicar he did not need to force conversation. Mr. Tellwright, after an inquiry as to whether the pullets were beginning to do their duty by the nation, and a confession that he knew nothing about hens, and had no desire for a *rapprochement*, let him alone to fill his pipe, and sit smoking and thinking in silence.

If Philipson had not been so preoccupied, he might have noticed that the Vicar also had something on his mind. But he did not. At supper they contrived between them to make a certain amount of conversation, though it was disjointed, and pauses were lengthy. Back in the study they settled down to chess with some thankfulness. But halfway through a game Mr. Tellwright, whose hand was stretched out to make a move. drew it back, and picking up one of Philipson's captured knights, began to finger the stiff frill of its mane.

"I'm sorry," he said, his eyes on the piece in his hand. "My mind isn't on the game. I have got something I must say to you."

He turned about in his chair and for a long time he said nothing, nor did he look at Philipson any more than Philipson looked at him.

"What is it?" Philipson asked at last, because he could not bear the silence any longer.

The Vicar half turned, glanced at him, and then away.

"I would like," he said, "to ask your pardon first. When I have finished you can give or refuse it as you like."

"What is it?" Philipson repeated sharply and rudely, but neither noticed anything strange in his tone.

"You'll have heard of course about this disappearance—old Marshall from Oldners Farm."

Philipson did not answer.

"Such a thing," the Vicar went on, "always starts a great deal of gossip, I suppose, in a village like this. Sometimes it's harmless gossip. Sometime it's—venomous. This time it's venomous."

He paused, as if he needed a question to help him on again, but Philipson did not supply it.

"Peppard, at the garage, is the originator of a certain story. I heard it through—I heard it, and I thought it my duty—though he does not come to church—but I think he goes nowhere—but as I am the representative of the Established Church——" Mr. Tellwright broke off; it was not time to debate the ethics of that question. "I went down to see him, and I reminded him of the risks of slander, and told him that if it were invoked by—by the aggrieved party he would find the consequences serious. But I regret to say," the Vicar's gentle voice faltered, "he maintained that this was not gossip —— And he has gone with his story to Sergeant Tucker. He——"

"What——" Philipson interrupted, and then had to clear his throat and begin again. "What is Peppard saying?"

Mr. Tellwright managed to tell him.

"Murder," Philipson repeated under his breath, not as a question, not as an exclamation, rather as if it were a word that was new to him, and whose significance he needed time to comprehend.

The Vicar, though he stared rigorously straight ahead, was yet conscious that Philipson's hands were thrust down between his knees, and so tightly locked together that they shook. He sat still, appalled. This was worse, incomparably worse than anything he had feared, for really he had not feared anything but acute embarrassment; he knew now that he had never really dreamed that the thing could be true.

The silence was so profound that the slightest sounds were obtrusive. As when he sat in his "Sermon Chair" groping for words to express the inexpressible, the Vicar heard the faint, tingling click of the hot coals in the grate, the flutter of flame, and the vibrating tick of the painted wall clock. These were peaceful and familiar sounds, but there was another which was neither. Philipson, sitting very still and rather crouching in the big crimson leather chair, was breathing as if he had run far and fast.

"I think," said Philipson suddenly, "that I'll go home. If you don't mind."

The Vicar got up. Neither looked at the other, but the Vicar spoke as he followed Philipson to the door.

"If I can help, I—I'm here."

"Thanks," said Philipson.

They passed out into the hall. Martha was going upstairs with hot water bottles. The Vicar lifted Philipson's coat from the peg.

"Did you come on your bike?" No one could have guessed from his voice that anything more disturbing than a game of chess had been taking place in the study.

Philipson responded better than might have been expected.

"No. I walked. It's cold tonight. It feels almost like snow."

The Vicar opened the door.

"Good night." Philipson passed him.

"Good night." The Vicar stepped out into the porch and stood listening to Philipson's footsteps; he was walking fast. Then Mr. Tellwright raised his eyes. The clouds were heavy. It was two hours before moonrise, and there was no gleam of any star.

10

PHILIPSON TRIES TO REMEMBER

THE GARDEN GATE at Miller's Green opened and shut
behind him with its usual scrape, wail, and click;
and Philipson went hastily up the path to the door. But even
before he reached it he guessed that Yorke was out, for there
was no light to be seen in any window, not even a chink, not
even that half-glow which the most meticulous disposer of
curtains is unable to stifle.

If Yorke was out, then the house was empty. Philipson remembered this just as the latchkey turned, and the realization
of it pulled him up in the dark, open doorway. For a good half
minute he simply did not dare to take the three steps forward
and stretch out his hand to the electric switch beside the sitting room door.

When at last he moved it was hurriedly. He switched on the
light, and went to the foot of the stairs.

"Yorke!" he shouted. "Yorke!" and was ashamed to hear his
voice pitched on such a high note. But no answer came.

He turned slowly to the front door, but he was unwilling to
shut it, because of the aversion he had for shutting himself
up in the empty house. It was black dark outside, very cold
and very quiet.

Suddenly the silence was broken by the harsh rattle of a

car just started up; the rattle changed to a rumbling purr, the purr to a steady, pulsing beat. The noise came from the garage; it must be Yorke's car, and he was not gone, but just going out.

Philipson took two steps out on to the path, then turned and bolted back into the house. If he ran round the front, he might miss Yorke. If he went out by the kitchen door he could cut him off, and now his one object was to stop Yorke going, or if he would not stop, to go out with him. Even if Yorke were driving over to Tetcot for bridge, and Philipson would have to tramp six miles back, he would have company for a little while. Anything was better than sitting in the empty house alone.

Mrs. Harker was one of those who believe that they who safe bind, safe find. One lock, two bolts and a chain had to be dealt with before Philipson could open the back door. He attacked them as if he were trapped in a burning house, and at last tore the door open, and ran out, and right up into the slowly moving blaze of the headlights, dazzled as blind as any rabbit along the road.

The car drew up with a quick grinding of brakes and a jerk that stopped the engine. Yorke shot out of the driver's seat, and in the sudden silence his voice sounded very loud.

"What the hell are you doing?"

Philipson, still unable to see, and peering stupidly, found it difficult, so challenged, to say just what he was doing, and why.

"What is the matter?" Yorke almost shouted at him. "I thought you were at the Vicarage."

"I came back."

"What for?"

"I—I—Where are you going?"

"Look here!" There was no doubt now that Yorke was angry.

Philipson hung fire over his explanation. Then he blurted out: "I'm sorry. I mean—I've had—a shock. I—the fact is, Yorke—I really can't bear to be alone for a bit."

"A shock? What do you mean?"

Philipson shut his mouth, and inwardly called himself a bloody fool. Then, in a sulky mumble—"I suppose I'll have to tell you."

Yorke did not answer; he seemed to be thinking hard. After a pause——

"All right. I'm not going to Tetcot. I'll be back soon. Then you can tell me."

"I'll come with you." Philipson made to open the door of the car, but Yorke waved him away.

"No. I'll put her back in the garage. You go into the house."

"But you were going out. I'll come too. I can talk to you on the way." He was quite determined not to be left alone.

Yorke had come round from the driving side. He almost shouldered Philipson away from the door.

"No. My business will—keep," he said, and laughed suddenly, but there was nothing of amusement in the laugh.

Philipson began to regret the solitude of the house. Yorke was clearly much put out, and of all people that he could have chosen, would, in that mood, be the worst to confide in.

Yorke came into the sitting room ostentatiously looking at his watch. This, thought Philipson, was going to be absolutely ghastly.

"Well," said Yorke, "what's up?"

He had not taken off his coat nor did he sit down, but stood, leaning an elbow on the chimney shelf. Philipson, gloomily studying Yorke's legs and feet, saw, without the fact meaning anything to him, that he was not wearing his exquisite evening black, and the patent leather shoes that were as glossy as garden slugs, but plus fours, and stout brogues.

"It's about—old Marshall." Philipson got the words out just in time to forestall Yorke's exclamation of impatience.

Yorke's fingers stopped their drumming on the chimney shelf.

"What about Marshall?"

"Peppard is saying I was up at Oldners Farm that afternoon."

"Peppard is saying—— Peppard? You? What do you

mean?" Yorke had dived his hands deep into his pockets. By the sound of his voice any one might guess that they were clenched. This impatience made it very difficult for Philipson; he grew confused—too confused to realize that he had begun his account from quite the wrong end.

"Tellwright told me," he said hastily. "He thought he ought to. He was jolly decent about it. He'd been to Peppard to tell him he'd better shut up. But Peppard said it wasn't gossip."

"Were you there? At Oldners Farm?"

The vehemence of Yorke's question pulled Philipson up short. He had to answer it. He caught one wrist with the other hand.

"I don't know," he said, "I can't remember."

"*You can't remember?* What do you mean?"

"I don't know—I can't remember—I don't know what I was doing that afternoon. I've forgotten." Philipson's voice cracked, but did not quite break. "I can't remember—— anything—for about three hours that day."

Yorke said, after quite a long pause: "Wait a minute." He went quickly out of the room. When he came back he was without his overcoat. He sat down now in his chair.

"You'd better tell me the whole thing."

He waited. But Philipson could not begin without help.

"What *do* you remember?" Yorke asked, impatience again in his voice.

"I know I started out. I remember that." Philipson frowned painfully into the fire. "I know Mrs. Harker wanted me to go to Marshall's about some honey. But I can't be sure if I remember her asking me, or if I know it because she told me afterwards that she had asked me. But I know I started out. I remember that." That solitary fact to which Philipson clung was, however, practically immaterial to the question.

"Yes, but what about the farm?" Yorke pressed him. "Were you—— Did you see—any one?"

"I tell you I can't remember. Except—— Wait a minute —— Just a minute."

The two men sat for a moment in utter silence; and Philip-

son at least was rigid with effort. "No," he gave a long sigh—
"I can't remember. I thought I remembered turning up the
Green Lane. But it's gone." He put his hands to his head. "I've
got such a headache," he said drearily.

Yorke was pouting and pinching his lips.

"Well what's the first thing you remember—after?"

Philipson shoved his clasped hands between his knees. This
was awful. Trying to remember that afternoon that he
couldn't remember hurt like fun. And now, after what the
Vicar had said, he was afraid to remember.

"I don't know what time it was," he began, slowly, "I was
back here." He nodded to his desk. "Sitting there. I don't
know how long I'd been there. I remember my hands felt
cold—uncomfortable and prickly you know. And I had got
out my handkerchief and I was drying them. So they must
have been wet. But I don't remember." He shook his head
and lapsed into silence.

"Well—and then?"

Philipson came back to the point with a jerk.

"I know I had a whacking headache. So when I'd dried
them I sat with my head in my hands holding it up. And I
saw Morgan's appointment card sticking out from a lot of
other things."

"You didn't go to Morgan's," Yorke put in quickly.

"No. I know I didn't. I got out the card and read it, and I
thought perhaps I'd had my tooth out, and that the gas had
made me—queer. But I felt round with my tongue and the
tooth was there still. So I knew I couldn't have been to
Morgan. I remember all that now, but somehow I forgot it
again that evening until you told me Morgan had rung up."

"So," Yorke summed it up, "you haven't the faintest idea
if you went to Oldners Farm or not?"

Philipson shook his head.

"I see," said Yorke, and then sat, pondering. Neither he nor
Philipson realized that only half the tale was out. "Have you
ever done this kind of thing before," Yorke said at last. "Lost
your memory, I mean?"

Philipson flinched. The subject had always been painful, and now it was like a nerve exposed.

"Yes." He forced himself to meet Yorke's stare. "In the war. I was shell-shocked—I went off my rocker for six months, about. But they said I was all right after, like other people, I mean."

"And you lost your memory then?" Yorke persisted.

Philipson wondered if he knew how it hurt to have to answer questions about all this. But he supposed Yorke meant to be kind, and that it had to be done.

"Yes," he said. "But it came back after."

"How soon?"

Philipson shook his head—"Bit by bit—I don't really know when. I remember nearly everything before I came out of hospital. They talk to you, you know," He explained vaguely.

Yorke said:

"Look here, Philipson, are you sure you can't remember? You can't remember anything?"

His voice surprised Philipson. He looked up. Yorke was leaning forward. Philipson had always thought his partner rather a selfish young blighter, but now the elegant and casually disdainful Yorke was quite obviously deeply interested, even moved. Philipson felt he had misjudged him; it was awfully decent of Yorke to be bothered with all this. But it was no good. He shook his head again.

"No, I can't. I can't."

But Yorke's eyes still held his and for some seconds the two men stared at each other. Then Philipson got hastily and clumsily to his feet.

"It's no good," he said, and put his hands to his head again. "It's no good. I can't remember. It's no good you trying to make me." He stopped, pulled himself together and spoke more quietly. "I think I'll go to bed," he said, and went.

It was perhaps ten minutes later that Yorke turned out the sitting room light and stepped into the dark hall.

"I say, Yorke!" Philipson spoke from upstairs, and switched on the landing light.

Yorke took his hand from the latch of the front door and

swung round. Philipson was standing on the stairs in his dressing gown and pyjamas.

"What is it?"

"While I was undressing I remembered——"

"Come down here! Come on!" Yorke turned on his heel and went quickly back into the sitting room. When Philipson had followed him in he shut the door and leaned his back against it.

"Now then. What have you remembered?"

"I forgot to tell you the rest of what Peppard is saying."

"Is that," said Yorke, "what you've remembered?"

"Yes—I mean—I only forgot when I was telling you."

"Oh! I see—— Well, get on. What is it?" He left the door and walked across to the fireplace, then came back to Philipson. "Well?" he said again.

Philipson shoved his hands into his dressing gown pockets because he did not want Yorke to see how they were shaking.

"Peppard is saying that—Marshall's been murdered."

"I know that." Yorke was very curt.

"And he's saying that I did it."

"You?" cried Yorke. "You?"

He had stepped back, and that sudden recoil taught Philipson the feelings of the leper. He himself moved away from Yorke.

"Yes—I see," he said, distractedly, hardly knowing what he was saying, "I know—I'd feel like that—— But—— Oh God! If I could remember! But I can't be sure——"

He was silent. They both were silent, and listened. The garden gate had opened and shut. There were heavy footsteps on the path.

"Mrs. Harker came in a little while ago." Philipson spoke in a whisper.

"You'd better clear out."

Philipson did not wait to be told again. He was halfway up the stairs before there was a knock at the front door.

Yorke came slowly out of the sitting room and opened to Sergeant Tucker.

11

TWO GENTLEMEN OBSTRUCT
THE POLICE

JUST TWO MINUTES after Philipson left the Vicarage Sergeant Tucker had arrived there, propped his bicycle against the wall of the porch, and plunged into that echoing and chilly cave, a monument, had he known it, to the influence of Ruskin, devised as it was on a scale suitable for containing a dozen lounging men-at-arms, as well as the bicycles of the Tellwright family and an ancient croquet set. Ruskin cropped up again and again throughout the house, in the awkward alliance between sash windows and Gothic arches, in the arrow slits (blocked) on either side of the larder ventilator, and in the stained glass which darkened the bath-room landing.

Sergeant Tucker stood for a moment in the draughty cave before hauling at the bell, which (Ruskin again) was neither of the modern nor of the Victorian type, but consisted of a black bar of iron run vertically through a series of stanchions, and ending below in a curve that was meant to recall a shepherd's crook.

Sergeant Tucker gave this mechanism a sharp pull, and listened to its variety of noises, for the fortuitous external creaking of the bar was almost as loud as the bell that jangled faintly within. In a moment he heard the footsteps of the Vicar's cook crossing the echoing tiles of the hall, and after a conflict with the massive bolts of the door, Martha looked out into the darkness.

"Evening, Martha," said Tucker.

"Oh! It's you. Good evening. How's Maggie?"

Martha flung the door wide. Unlike Mrs. Harker she always found something exhilarating in a policeman; and besides, Tucker's wife was her second cousin.

"All right, thanks. Can I see the Vicar?"

Martha said: "Step inside, I'll shut the door. This house is like a tomb even in midsummer. I'll see. I know he's alone, because Mr. Philipson has just gone."

"Mr Philipson?"

Martha stopped on her way to the study door.

"Yes—he's just gone. You must have passed him in the road."

"I did meet someone," said Tucker. "Was he in a hurry?" The man he had met had gone by without the usual country "good night."

"May be. He left early anyhow." Martha diverted her attention from Tucker, and concentrated it on the door of the study.

"Come in!" said the Vicar's voice.

When Mr. Tellwright heard that it was Sergeant Tucker who wanted to see him, his heart gave a most unpleasant jump. His first thought: "He's come for Philipson," was manifestly absurd. His second: "He's come to collect evidence," was almost as daunting, and nearer to likelihood. But in the two or three seconds during which he listened to the approaching clank of Sergeant Tucker's boots, Mr. Tellwright sharply called his mind to order. It simply could not be true. Things like that didn't happen. The sight of Sergeant Tucker, large, solid, and familiar, assisted him in this hasty re-establishment of equilibrium.

"Come in, Sergeant!" He pulled a chair—Philipson's chair —a few inches nearer to the fire. "Sit down." Of course it was all right, he told himself again, but his fine ear detected in his own voice a note of false heartiness.

Sergeant Tucker heard nothing amiss. He was fully occupied by the necessity for making a decision, a sudden decision, and Tucker was a slow man. He had come to the Vicarage to announce to the Vicar that once more Ben Wilkinson had been run in, drunk and disorderly, leaving a motherless family of eight to fend for itself. But when Martha had mentioned Mr. Philipson it had seemed, he thought, providential like. Mr. Philipson was much on his mind. He would like to speak of him to the Vicar. But could he?

Mr. Tellwright, all unaware of Tucker's dilemma, gave him time to decide. Though always accessible, and above all a good listener, the Vicar was not usually a chatty man. But this evening he had so much to say about the weather, and its effects upon crops, gardens, the health of the parish, old Archer's rheumatism, and the sale of motor cars, that for more than five minutes Tucker had no need to say more than yes, and no, and indeed sir.

At last, however, Mr. Tellwright paused. He realized that, since he could not talk Tucker out of the house, he had better let him do his worst. But while talking, he also had been facing a decision, and his more agile mind had been capable of reaching it in spite of his conversational efforts.

"Now, Sergeant," he broke off, and asked the question with a kind of desperate jocularity: "What crime have I been committing?"

Tucker's nerves were in far too good order to cause him to jump, but this opening, so apt to one of his preoccupations, did startle him.

He smiled politely and rumbled something appreciative of the Vicar's little joke, then became portentously grave.

"Well, sir," he said, "I really came about Ben Wilkinson. Had to run him in again, same as usual. I thought you'd like to know because of the kids. But there's another thing I'd like to talk to you about."

The Vicar sat very still.

"People talk so in a little place like this," said Tucker.

Mr. Tellwright, hearing his own opening gambit so closely echoed, was again, in mind, staring into the fire, yet knowing that Philipson sat opposite, his head bowed, his fingers picking at the worn leather on the arm of the chair As if someone else was speaking he heard his own voice saying judicially:

"Very mischievous gossip too sometimes—and without a crumb of truth in it."

Tucker's face brightened.

"Just what I say, sir."

Mr. Tellwright was filled with a sudden flush of quite inexplicable excitement. He felt frightened; he felt guilty; a thing hard, heavy, and cold as a stone lay darkly at the bottom of his mind; and yet he was enjoying this. It was a game. He must play it.

"Are you perhaps," he went on, "alluding to the tale which I hear Peppard is so injudiciously spreading in Benmarsh?"

"You've heard it?" Tucker was vastly relieved. He would not now have to tell the Vicar.

"I have. And I went and warned him of the existence of a law against slander."

"He's a damn' meddling busybody!" Sergeant Tucker trumpeted suddenly, and added: "Begging your pardon, sir."

The Vicar inclined his head. Then, wrenching his eyes from Tucker and fixing them upon the tips of his fingers, he said: "I thought it my duty to tell Mr. Philipson of these stories."

Tucker in his heart blessed the Vicar and his stars that he had broached the subject. "And what did he say, sir? If I may ask."

Mr. Tellwright looked quickly at him.

"I didn't ask him to say anything," he said.

Tucker felt rebuked. "Of course not. Of course not," he mumbled hastily. Then: "It's all rot to my way of thinking, just tommyrot. If Peppard had seen Mr. Philipson *going* to the farm it would have been another kettle of fish. But— Ipsden Woods! Why there's nothing to show that Mr. Philipson'd been near Oldners Farm. And that part about blood on his hands is all my eye." He snorted with indignation. "I'll see Peppard again, and tell him to shut his blooming head! If you'll excuse me saying so," he added hastily.

He got up as if he would go and see Peppard at once, and the Vicar did not detain him. At the door Tucker remembered again the predicament of the Wilkinson children, but that transaction took no time. Mr. Tellwright would certainly see to it.

In the porch Tucker paused and turned back.

"Thank you, sir," he said in the low rumble that was the nearest he could get to a whisper. "I'm very glad to have had this talk with you. Of course, as a matter of form I'll have to ask Mr. Philipson whether he went to Marshall's that day."

"Yes," said Mr. Tellwright. "Of course."

"I'm sorry to trouble him at all. But it's only a matter of form. I had to ask Mr. Yorke too. He did go up there that day, but he saw no one."

"Oh well," said Mr. Tellwright, and did not know whether it were his own or Philipson's tracks he was covering. "No innocent man minds answering a question like that."

All the same when Sergeant Tucker presented himself at the door of Miller's Green, he felt far from comfortable. He was almost glad, though certainly it did not help his quest, that it was Mr. Yorke who opened the door.

Was Mr. Philipson in, inquired the Sergeant, and was afraid it was rather late to call.

Yes—Philipson was in, Yorke told him. "But he went up to bed—oh—may be twenty minutes ago; as soon as he came in, in fact. I don't know if he's asleep yet. Is it anything particular? If you don't mind me asking."

Tucker indicated rather confusedly that he didn't mind. "There's no light upstairs," he said in a disappointed tone. "So I suppose he's asleep."

"Hm—Yes. Probably. But I'll call him up, shall I?"

Yorke moved to the stairway, but Tucker said something, and he stopped.

"What d'you say?"

Tucker said he didn't want to disturb Mr. Philipson. It could keep. But he did not say good night.

"Can I help?" Mr. Yorke asked politely.

Tucker looked doubtful.

Yorke came back to the door.

"Look here. Is it about this—this nonsense of Peppard's?"

Tucker, with apology in his voice, admitted that it was.

"Well," said Yorke tartly, "I never heard such damned rot. Philipson's very much upset about it. Any one would be. Beastly thing to have said about you. I'd be mad as blazes!"

Tucker hastily disassociated himself from those who had upset Mr. Philipson; he only wanted to ask him, as a matter of form, whether he'd been to Oldners Farm that afternoon at all.

"I know he didn't." Yorke was emphatic. "Funny thing is that he ought to have gone. He promised Mrs. Harker to go about some honey on his way to the dentist. The funny old bird started off and d'you know, he simply funked it—the dentist, I mean. Instead of going to Mallingford he went walking round I don't know where. Felt frightfully ashamed of himself, and I don't wonder. I've been ragging him about it no end."

Sergeant Tucker laughed; it seemed to be expected of him, and laughter comes easily from a lightened heart. This was just the kind of explanation—idiotic, trivial, convincing—that he had needed to discount Peppard's wild tale.

"So that's that," he said and chuckled again, "I needn't trouble Mr. Philipson."

Yorke opened the door again, and stepped outside with the Sergeant. The light shone out on a dizzying descending drift of white flakes in the darkness.

"Snow, by Jove!" said Tucker.

Yorke said nothing, but after Tucker and he had bade each other a cordial good night, he stood for a moment watching the fall.

"Gad!" he ejaculated, as though this atmospheric phenomenon both surprised and pleased him. Then he shut the door.

Philipson heard the sound, and moved from his place of

concealment beside the big linen press on the landing. On tiptoe he came to the top of the stairs. As he peered down Yorke looked up.

"Oh!" said Yorke. "You were listening, were you?"

Philipson was clearly much ashamed, but he did not try to excuse himself.

"It's most awfully good of you, Yorke," he said. He came downstairs, and passing Yorke went into the sitting room. Yorke followed him, but did not shut the door. "Aren't you going to bed?" he asked.

Philipson had begun to walk up and down the length of the room. He did not seem to hear Yorke's question. Yorke repeated it.

"What? Going to bed? No—not yet. It's no use—I shan't sleep." He continued his tramping. Yorke moved towards the door.

"No," cried Philipson sharply. "Don't go! I must talk to you."

He did not look at his partner and so missed the expression with which Yorke regarded him. He had indeed quite forgotten that Yorke was still waiting to go out; he only remembered how kind he had been.

"It is decent of you," he repeated. "But it's no good, you see," he rambled on, thinking aloud. "Not really. Though I can't tell you how grateful I am to you for getting rid of Sergeant Tucker. For of course I *may* remember at any moment, I suppose, and it may—be all right. But if—it's true —then——" he spread out his hands. "If it's true——" he said again, and seemed to shrink into a yet smaller, greyer, more insignificant little man.

Yorke interrupted brusquely.

"Look here, Philipson," he said. "You just get off to bed. And listen to me. Whether you've done it or not, keep out of Tucker's way for the next few days—or if you meet him, tell him just what I told him. But I think you're a poor liar, and so you'd better keep out of his way. Stay in the house. I'll say you've got a cold."

Philipson looked at his partner with something of a dumb protest in his eyes.

"But——" he began, then gave that up. "Yes. I see what you mean. I suppose you're right."

"And now," said Yorke, and could not keep the impatience out of his voice, "get off to bed, for heaven's sake!"

Philipson caught the inflection and remembered suddenly. "Oh I say, I'm sorry," he apologized hastily, "I'd forgotten you were going out. But I suppose I've kept you too late now. Or are you going?"

Yorke did not look at him.

"It's too late," he said. "I'll have to go out to the garage though and run the engine a bit to warm her. So if you hear anything you'll know that no one's stealing the car." He took a book from the shelves, and dropped into his chair.

"Good night," he said with finality.

For perhaps twenty minutes after Philipson had gone upstairs he sat with the book on his knee. Then he got up, and went out into the hall. He stood for a moment listening, opened the front door, and stepped out upon the path.

Snow crunched under his feet. The moon was behind clouds, but the garden had a pale glow of its own from the light but unbroken drift of white that covered it. The fall had ceased and the air was still and sharp with frost. Yorke stood looking out for a while, then went back into the house, and to the sitting room. He sat down again to his book, but every now and again he got up, pulled the curtains aside, and looked out. It was after midnight when he shoved the book back into its place in the shelf, and took a last look at the night.

The world lay covered with snow, immaculate. A cat, quiet as a shadow, stole across the garden. For a moment its eyes gleamed green as it turned them towards the lighted window. The clouds were breaking; a star or two showed. There would be no more snow tonight. Yorke went slowly up to bed.

12

PHILIPSON SEARCHES
FOR BLOODSTAINS

NEXT MORNING PHILIPSON came late into the bathroom. The night had been awful, but nothing seems so black in the morning, and this morning was a marvel of untouched exquisite whiteness under a sky of softly blue as if the heat of summer filled it. He pushed open the bathroom window; like the overflowing of a deep well the air rushed in, pure of all scents, clean, and sharply cold. Away in the field he could see the chickens, the copper coloured burning against the snow, the white looking yellow almost as butter. Even from this distance he could see the February redness of the cocks' combs and hackles, bright as pimpernels, full of the life of spring. At the sight of those colours, so vivid in the midst of a blue and white world, Philipson's heart, like pilgrim Christian, "gave three jumps for joy." He leaned against the washbasin under the window looking out, and because he did not want to take his eyes from the sight he fumbled round with his hand for the hot tap. His fingers found it, and turned it on, and the water began its subdued song as it ran down into the basin.

Suddenly he drew in his head. The pleasure that the colours

had wakened faded from his eyes. Horror grew there instead.

He stood for minutes, watching the water running from the
tap. It circled and twisted in a plait of transparent shining
lines, narrowing and fining down till it reached the plug hole.
The sound of the water, and the sight of it, and the red combs
of the cocks—— He raised his hands and clasped his fore-
head.

He had washed his hands here a few days ago, and had
stood, watching the water running off gurgling into the plug
hole. But the water had been red.

He went away from the basin and sat on the edge of the
bath. He remembered that red water clearly, though he remembered nothing of what came before or what followed
after. But he had stood by the basin, and seen red water run
away down the pipe. It must have been on that afternoon—on
Tuesday afternoon.

So it was true.

For a long time he sat quite still, and his mind too was still,
and cowering. But after a while reason, or will, or perhaps
only the dumb instinct of self-preservation stirred. He began
to say to himself that he wasn't sure yet. He sat up straighter
on the edge of the bath.

But the remembrance came back fresh and startling into his
mind, and he shrank again from it, and felt sick. Yet he wasn't
sure. Well, he must make sure.

He got up, and found himself stumbling against the washbasin. That startled and humiliated him; he gritted his teeth
together and started again. This time he managed to go
straight, if jerkily, along the passage to his own bedroom. He
went in and shut the door behind him, and then stood still
and felt his face cold, and the sweat running down his back
under his pyjamas.

What he had to do now was to search his clothes for blood-
stains. In murder trials the police always did it. He must do
it for himself.

With more courage than he gave himself credit for, he
began systematically to consider what clothes he had worn on
that day. It hadn't been very cold. Grey slacks then, and if

grey slacks the newest pair, since he had been going to Milling-
ford. He found the trousers and tossed them on to the bed,
and began to rummage among his coats. It would have been
this coat; so it joined the trousers on the bed and a waistcoat
followed. What else? Socks. Shirt. He dug into the soiled linen
basket. He couldn't possibly remember which of these he had
worn, so he must look through all the socks and shirts.

He did so, methodically. The search was steadying his
nerves. The knowledge of what hung upon the issue retired
to the back of his mind. And there was nothing incriminating
on any of the soiled underclothes. He thrust them back into
the basket, and flapped the lid shut.

Next he examined the waistcoat and coat. Nothing there.
He took up the trousers and looked them over, and his heart
gave a jolt. There was a mark on the grey flannel at the left
knee, a stiff stain of dark brown like chocolate.

He laid the trousers down again on the bed and stood staring at them. He had been looking for a stain, and here was
one. But something obstinate in his mind began to argue. It
might not be a bloodstain. If it were a bloodstain it might be
his own blood; perhaps he had cut his finger. He spread out
both his hands and looked them over carefully. There was a
half-healed scar on his left thumb. He could not remember
when or how he had cut it, but it was fairly deep, and must
have bled a good bit.

His eyes went back to the trousers. It was a bloodstain.
Everything, like stiff fingers pointing, seemed to turn him
back to that horror from which he shrank.

But still—he was not certain, and he began to find in himself a craving for one thing—certainty. Even if it were certainty of the the worst it would be better than this. But how
could he find out?

As he stood there, leaning his knees against the edge of the
bed, an obscure and incomplete memory began to stir in him.
He'd read a book once, he couldn't remember the title or the
author, or even the story, but before the eyes of his mind there
became visible, as if he had actually seen them while he read
the book, a pair of white canvas tennis shoes. Someone in the

story had worn them; it might have been the murderer, or the man he had murdered; but somehow, in the story, by means of those white canvas shoes, the crime had been discovered.

His shoes were in the cupboard by the window, all tumbled anyhow, as he kept most of his possessions. He scooped them out and sat back on his heels to think. It was very hard to remember which pair of shoes he had worn that day, but after consideration he reduced the possibilities to two pairs. He tossed the others back, and then he lifted up one of those he had left out.

As he looked at it he saw that one of the laces had been broken and knotted. Something like a small electric shock seemed to touch his brain. Yes—— He remembered tying that knot. He remembered breaking the lace, and swearing, and thinking to himself that it was just the kind of thing that would happen to a fellow when he was going to the dentist. He had tied that knot before he started out on Tuesday, but—— God!—what had happened before he came home?

He sat down on the floor and began to look over the pair. There was nothing that he could see upon the left shoe. He let it tumble off his knee and picked up the other. But he was beginning to think that this was a silly thing to be doing. Whatever could there be on a shoe? As he turned it over in his hand he was thinking—"I'll have to have them heeled soon anyway."

His eyes, trained not only to look, but also to see, caught sight of something in the angle between heel and sole. He bent closer. Then he put the shoe down beside him, very gently, and got out his penknife. It took him a long time to open it, because his fingers were unsteady.

He lifted the shoe again, put the point of the penknife under the small fragment by the heel, lifted it off, and laid it on his palm.

A blow like a hammer fell upon his brain. He sat staring at the thing on his palm, but he had to drop the penknife and hold one wrist with the other hand because it shook too much to support that tiny thing, like a bit of broken eggshell, caked and smeared with dark brown, and sticking to it three short, greyish hairs.

Yorke was by the open front door, looking out at the garden, when Philipson, still in his dressing gown and slippers, came downstairs. He turned, saw Philipson's face in the clear bright light, and stood staring at him. Philipson had something in his hand; he carried it, as a boy will carry a bird's egg for safety, in one palm and covered with the other. He seemed to be trying to speak but Yorke could not hear that he said anything.

"Come in here." Yorke used almost the same words that he had used last night, and as last night, when Philipson followed him into the room he shut the door behind them.

"What is it?" he asked.

Philipson said nothing, but he stretched his hands forward towards Yorke, and took away the covering one.

Yorke could see that something lay in the cupped palm, but he could not see what it was.

"What the hell is it?" he asked.

Philipson stuck out his hand at the full stretch of his arm, and strained his head away from it, like a woman measuring a yard of silk between her finger ends and her chin.

Yorke, stooping over the stiffly extended hand, saw now what it was that lay there. It was a little splinter of bone clotted with brown blood, and stuck with a few short grey hairs.

"Take it!" cried Philipson suddenly, and then, his voice rising higher and higher. "Take it! Take it! Take it!"

He tipped his hand over blindly, and blundered away across the room. He flopped down in his chair, seemed to be going to hide his face in his hands, but snatched them away, rolled over, and buried it instead in the cushion.

Yorke had instinctively put out his hand to catch the thing as Philipson had emptied it away, and now he stood looking down at it as it lay in his own palm. His face whitened. He did not need to ask what it was. He knew.

"Where did you find it?"

After a minute Philipson's voice—only it was not in the least like Philipson's voice—told him: "On my shoe—by the heel."

Yorke moved quickly across the room to the fireplace. Mrs. Harker's fires were no sulky heaps of coal, feathered with smoke and garnished with small flickers of flame; they were royal, red-hearted furnaces by the time the gentlemen were down to their breakfasts. Yorke emptied the bit of bone into the hottest part of the fire. He heard a little sharp splutter. The thing was gone.

"What have you done with it?" Philipson asked from behind him.

"I've burnt it." Yorke's voice was savage.

"The police—will want it."

"Well, they can't have it."

Kindness comes with disabling force to a desperate man. Philipson had found Yorke unexpectedly, inexplicably kind last night, but this went beyond. He put his hand up to his mouth and bit hard on it. When he spoke it was in a sort of gasp.

"You're frightfully—decent—not to—— You oughtn't——"

Yorke turned round and stared at him. His expression was one of pure surprise at first. Then it changed. Philipson's face was crumpled like a bit of white paper. A tear was trickling down one cheek. Yorke was filled with a fury of scorn. He could have yelled abuse at the creature sitting there with its face quivering. He turned sharply away to the window.

After a few moments Philipson said, in a voice that sounded as if he had worn it out with shouting:

"Ought I to go to Tucker and tell him?"

"No!" Yorke almost yelled at him.

"All right," Philipson agreed meekly. "What shall I do?"

Yorke realized with something of a shock that Philipson would do exactly as he said. Incredible, comical as it was, the fellow thought that he was being shielded, and was grateful. But what to tell him to do? Yorke must think.

"Don't you be such a fool," he said roughly. "Don't go outside the house today. I'll see to the chickens. I'll tell Mrs.

Harker you've got a cold—or toothache—or something——
But I must think—I must think."

He was pacing up and down the room. His friends would
hardly have recognized the airily supercilious Marc Yorke.
Certainly Philipson found him, in this sympathetic agitation,
almost a stranger. But whatever his surprise might be concerning Yorke his thoughts were diverted by a sudden and
overwhelming desire to sneeze. He sneezed, shivered, and said
mournfully:

"I've managed to get a cold all right. I suppose I'd better
go up and dress."

Yorke agreed, but his attention was clearly elsewhere.
When Philipson had gone he stood by the window for a long
time staring out, his expression one of intense concentration.
Yet his eyes noticed and followed the line of little footmarks
that crossed the white garden, puncturing it with soft shadows, the trail of that same prowling cat which had gone by
as he stood at the door last night. Even from the window he
could trace the slot, out of the Japanese Rugosa bushes, over
the grass, and into the holly hedge on the opposite side.

With this snow, this damned snow, a cat couldn't cross the
garden without leaving its track, still less could a man cross
an untrodden field. And now Philipson, who had twice
stopped Yorke's going out when the going had been good, was
like a live bomb with the time fuse set at an unknown figure.
It was certain that he had been to Oldners Farm that afternoon, and any moment he might remember what he must
have seen there. If he did remember, Sergeant Tucker would
soon know what had become of old Marshall. Whatever happened, Sergeant Tucker must not know that, for once he
knew, the hunt would be up.

Mrs. Harker's footsteps sounded in the hall. After the dis-
creetest shadow of a knock upon the door, she opened and
looked in.

Would Mr. Philipson be down to breakfast, she asked, in
a grey and disapproving tone.

"Yes," said Yorke briskly. "He won't be long now. He

thinks he's starting a cold. I've just been dosing him with quinine. He'll have to stay in today."

"Thank you, sir."

Mrs. Harker retired. She had no kindness for Mr. Philipson, but she would have been surprised had she known, that just as she closed the door, Mr. Yorke reached the conclusion that his partner must die.

13

YORKE GETS READY A PISTOL

About half an hour later Yorke put his head inside the dining room while Philipson was eating a very belated breakfast.

"You might," he said hastily, and without looking at Philipson. "You might have a go at the books this morning as you're staying in the house. I shall be busy." He shut the doors without waiting for a reply.

It was a perfect day. The sun shone out of a cloudless sky upon trees and hedges dressed with a light powdering of frozen snow. The elms stood up like enormous fruit trees burdened on every twig with white blossom, high in the blue and shining air. The snow was so dry and powdery that even the best efforts of the school children could not mould it into snowballs; they could only pelt each other with white spray. It was a day to thank God for, but Marc Yorke went about his business without any sensations of gratitude.

All morning, as he went round the fields and chicken houses, one question was hammering his brain—how to kill a man so that it seemed that the man had killed himself? The very urgency of the matter was making it difficult for him to think connectedly. He had constantly to push out of his mind the knowledge of the risk he ran—the hideous risk he had chosen to run. He had thought himself so clever, that Tuesday afternoon. The concealment of Marshall's carcase had been almost a joke, so clever had he thought himself. But now he was frightened.

Indoors Philipson was hardly in better case. He was never a good hand either at correspondence or accounts, and these were usually Yorke's part of the business. Today, with a mind distracted, he was a hopeless bungler. He calculated, and re-calculated, the weekly cost of chicken food during the last month, and found its fluctuations inexplicable until he realized that at times he was dividing hundredweights by shillings, and at times multiplying them by days. Yet, though it gradually was borne in upon him that the chicken farm would be better served should he refrain from further disastrous efforts, and cease to wear away the pages of the account books by repeated scratchings-out with a penknife, he continued doggedly to labour over the accounts; anything was better than to have to sit still and to think. It was, consequently, with considerable relief, that he heard Agnes come out of the kitchen and play her solo upon the dinner gong.

Yorke came into the dining room with *The Times* under his arm, and spread it out, and hid himself behind it. It was not that he cared what the Prime Minister had been saying, or what the Labour Party had been deploring, or who had been to the Arts Ball; but he did not want to have to talk. It was becoming all he could do to pretend to be the ordinary cool, casual, disdainful Marc Yorke, while, behind the disguise, and in his brain, was a wild beast that thrashed about and raged; a beast that was a little bit mad with fear.

To add to the strain which he had to endure, Philipson's cold was now no future possibility, but a lamentable fact, and human beings are abject things when they suffer from a running cold. Philipson sat humped in his chair, breathing heavily through his mouth; now and then he snuffed slightly, now and then he trumpeted into his handkerchief. Yorke could hardly bear to look at him; he felt towards his partner as a squeamish child feels towards a repulsive insect which must, somehow, be squashed.

But because he could not help it he lowered *The Times* an inch, and looked across the top at Philipson, who, at that moment, was raising on his fork a mouthful of liver and bacon. A sudden thought, humorous yet grotesque, alleviated Yorke's distress. It was indeed rather odd to be having lunch with a man, and to be wondering all the time just how that machine—busy now putting liver and bacon into its mouth, mincing it with teeth, and digesting it with ingeniously de-signed organs lower down—it really was odd to be wondering just how that machine could be smashed and put out of action for ever.

That thought restored him. Like a sudden wave lifting and running in through his mind, he felt an enormous, swelling confidence in himself. The wave turned over and broke, glori-ously. He would do it, somehow. He was sure he could. Old Marshall was nothing; Philipson was nothing, but he, Marc Yorke, was a man of power. He could have laughed aloud if he had been alone.

The lessening of the strain brought such relief that he felt suddenly almost friendly towards Philipson, and began to talk confidently, openly, of the thing he had been secretly considering in his mind. "I must clean my guns this after-noon," he said. The fool opposite would never guess what would be the mark of one of those guns, if only, if only Yorke could think of a way to make the murder look like self-mur-der.

Philipson came out of his thoughts with a jerk. "I'll do it for you—I rather like"—he stopped to sneeze, and then went on—"doing that sort of thing."

Thought, as Hobbes remarked, is quick. During the time it took Philipson to sneeze Mr. Yorke had found a way by which, with luck, not only would the fool opposite seem to have shot himself, but actually would have shot himself. As Philipson finished his sentence Yorke saw him lying on the floor between the door and the window, Yorke's automatic in his hand, oil and emery powder spilt on the floor, and blood, from a hole in Philipson's head, slowly mixing with them.

"Oh don't bother, thanks," he said, "I expect I'll have time before I go out." ·

Yorke, who resented mess when made by others, was much less pernickety when he made it himself. After lunch he spread newspapers over the sitting-room table and brought out his guns and began to clean them. While he worked on them Philipson sat down dispiritedly to read a book; Yorke looked across at him from time to time, again savouring an unusual situation—it was interesting to sit and look at a man with a gun in your hand and wonder if you could shoot him just so that it would look like suicide. But the other way— Yorke bent over the gun he held—the other way was much safer.

When he had cleaned the two guns, he leaned back in his chair.

"That's done. I don't think the automatic needs cleaning." He picked it up from the table and cast his eye first on Philipson, then on the pistol. "Damn!" he said loudly.

Philipson looked round. Yorke was stooping over the table.

"That cupboard room must be damp. There's rust in the barrel. I'll have to do it after all."

He slid out the magazine, and tipped the cartridges, one by one, out on the table, counting aloud as they dropped. "One, two, three, four, five, six, seven, eight. That's the lot." Philipson was certainly not absorbed in his book; he ruffled the pages and yawned; now he looked over his shoulder again as the little things tapped out on the wood. Yorke laid the magazine down, and peered earnestly up the barrel of the pistol, then he glanced from it to the clock.

"Gosh!" he exclaimed. "Nearly a quarter to three! I simply must go. What an infernal nuisance! I wanted to finish this before I went. Can't think how this rust got in. Never knew it before. . . ." He stopped his muttering because Philipson had moved; he laid his book down on the rug and got up.

"Let's see," he said. He came over to Yorke and held out his hand for the pistol. "I'll clean it for you."

Yorke flourished it at him. "See that bit of rust?" he said

and took it away again, leaving Philipson with his hand still stretched out. Then he jumped up, still holding the pistol.

"Will you really? It would be awfully good of you. Half a minute! I'll get you the cleaning rod." He dashed out of the room, slamming the door.

In the cupboard room there was an old chest. Very quietly, and listening all the time, Yorke laid the pistol down, lifted the lid of the chest, found first the cleaning rod, then the box of cartridges. He took one out.

"Now, careful!" he muttered to himself.

He slid the breech back, slipped the cartridge into the chamber, and let the breech slide gently home again. The thing was done.

When he went back to the sitting room he had his coat over his arm and his hat in his hand. Philipson was standing by the table. He was fingering the locks of Yorke's shot guns. He was nothing of a shot but the cold iron was grateful to his hot fingers; so was the exact workmanship of the mechanism to his craftsman's eye.

Yorke put the pistol and cleaning rod down on the table.

"There it is. Thanks awfully. Put the cartridges back when you've finished will you. They're all there." He reached across, barring Philipson's approach to the pistol, and again counted out the eight cartridges. "That's right," he said. "So long." He snatched up his hat and made for the door.

As he shut it after him he looked back. Philipson was tipping out some emery powder. He had the cleaning rod in his other hand.

Yorke slammed the door behind him and fairly bolted across the front of the house. He fetched up at the garage blown and panting, though it was a small distance, threw himself into the car and feverishly pressed the self-starter. When the engine roared into life he was thankful, as if for a reprieve. This would cover the concussion of that shot which he dared not hear.

Yet when he drove the car out and turned into the road his heart was high and orgulous. It was clever. It was clever. It needed only a bit of luck—and he believed again that his luck

was in—and at any moment now Philipson, peering into the
barrel of a pistol whose magazine had been emptied before
his eyes, trying to clean away a piece of rust which did not
exist, would touch off the trigger.

It was half an hour perhaps, before Yorke came back from
the village where he had bought stamps, and tobacco, and
talked to quite a number of people. As he passed the sitting-
room window he glanced in, but the room seemed to be
empty. His spirits fell with a jar—could it have failed? But
surely it couldn't.

He hung up his coat in the hall. He made himself behave in
a perfectly normal way. Then he came back to the sitting
room and opened the door.

The first thing he saw was the automatic lying on the floor.
A chair was pushed askew. From under the table a pair of
grey-trousered legs stuck stiffly out.

"Good God!" he shouted.

The legs gave a convulsive kick. The body twisted itself
about on the floor, and Philipson's face appeared from under
the table.

"What's the matter?" he asked, and then as if some explanation was necessary. "One of the beastly cartridges has
got itself wedged under the skirting. I upset the box."

Yorke had shut the door behind him. He came quickly
across the room and swept up the pistol from the floor. He
saw that Philipson, on his knees now, was watching him.

"I thought—you'd shot yourself." Yorke turned away, but
he could not properly control his voice.

Philipson gave a forced, embarrassed laugh. Yorke's obvious emotion had touched him very near. "Not this time," he
said idiotically, and added hastily, to break the strained
silence:

"I'm sorry I haven't even cleaned it. Tellwright came in
just after you'd gone, for a subscription. And then—I don't
know—I was just——"

But the end of his explanation missed its mark. Yorke had
gone noisily out. Philipson was left to reflect upon the fact
that both Mr. Tellwright and Yorke had been equally con-

vinced that he would, as a matter of course, be intending to commit suicide.

Yorke went up to his bedroom, shut the door, and then shoved the pistol into the drawer in which his collars lay in glossy concentric rings. Then he began to tramp up and down the length of that delicately furnished room, with its lovely old half tester and the embroidered quilt of green silk, and the Japanese prints, the framed eighteenth century embroideries and the long, low shelf of books. This thing wasn't a game any longer; he had ceased to believe in his luck, and outside, in the shining serenity of the day, horribly decked with snow, was that wreck of old Marshall, visible to any one who went that way, and for Yorke as remote and unattainable as the moon itself. He was very, very frightened.

After some time, he did not know how long, he checked himself, and stood still. If Mrs. Harker were in the kitchen, she might hear his footsteps, and wonder. He must avoid anything unusual. He dug his nails into his palms, stood quite still, and with an enormous effort, beat down the panic that was rising in him. But as he brought that under, something else grew and swelled in his mind. Hate for Philipson towered up like a thundercloud; it was enormous; it filled him; he felt his mind might burst with it.

14

THE BODY IS STILL THERE

ONLY ONE OF the windows at Oldners Farm looked towards the south and the main road, and that was an attic window. The farm had been built before builders and farmers made any account of sunshine for human beings, therefore the house faced to the north and the long slow rise of Footpad Hill, cut through with a cart track that ran straight up between a cluster of stacks, a Dutch barn, and, just now, some movable hen houses. Between the stacks hung an inspiriting display of dead rooks, looped like festival decorations across the cart road. In a high wind the whole swag swung to and fro, and the individual carcases twisted slowly round. Sometimes one of them fell down with a thump.

As a consequence of the northerly aspect of the house, Mrs. Marshall, unless she went up into the attic, could not see one particular field which lay to the southeast of the house and which was in her mind night and day. Since Tuesday she had made the ascent every morning, and sometimes, although, as it were, against her will, more than once during the day. But each time the thing was there; Mr. Yorke's promise was still unfulfilled; the fear and the horror in Mrs. Marshall's mind still unrelieved. Today, as she climbed the steep flight of attic stairs, which the white light off the snow made unusually bright, she had great hope that surely this time the thing would be gone and the field empty and innocent under its new coverlet of white. That hope was not induced merely by the natural reaction of human nature to bright sunshine, pure colour, and keen air. Mrs. Marshall had given her imagination more exercise during the past few days than at any time since the years of her sulky and discontented girlhood. For hours of each night she had lain awake, trying and to some extent succeeding in imagining what might happen, sometimes with hope, sometimes with despair and a freezing fear. Waking early this morning with a full moon staring her in the face, she had gone barefoot to her window and looked out on the snow. Back again in bed, her cold feet in her hands, she had constructed an imaginary release from her dread. Last night, she told herself, before the snow fell—and it hadn't started to fall before ten o'clock because she'd looked through the window after she blew out her candle—last night Mr. Yorke had come and taken away that thing in the field, and then the snow had fallen and covered the place where it had been— like oblivion. That was the thought in her mind, though the word was unknown to her; but it meant that there would be no more fear of questions from Sergeant Tucker, nor of Joe taking it into his head to go into that field—no more of this peering out of windows and cowering in the house; the business would in fact be over and she could push it out of her mind and forget. She was sure she would soon forget.

Consequently, when she saw that the thing was still there, and more than ever apparent, indeed to her blatantly, ostentatiously, visible, the burden of fear was harder to bear than ever before. She felt that as the thing was still there today, so it never would be moved. What was Mr. Yorke doing? He had told her to say nothing, to do nothing, to wait. But he had done nothing either. She gripped her cold fingers together and leaned against the little window, the smell of frost and the smell of the dusty rag of lace curtain that hung there, mingling in her nostrils. She found herself whispering the dirtiest words she knew to describe him. The thought ran through her like a red-hot needle that she hated him now; it hardly surprised her to realize that she had hated him for quite a long time.

She wished, with a pang which sickened her, that he'd never come near the place. And he never would have come, he'd said so himself, if it hadn't been for that Mr. Philipson painting his silly old picture of her. So it was really all Mr. Philipson's fault. "It was." Mrs. Marshall muttered the words half aloud in the silence of the house: "It *was* his fault."

But she knew it was not, for her passionate longing to undo what was done had taken her mind back to the first time that Yorke had come to Oldners Farm. One evening last November, almost at dark, someone had knocked at the door. She had opened, and seen a stranger standing outside, with a gun over his shoulder and some limp pheasants dangling from his hand. He had come to ask his way by the short cut through the fields. "Peppard had told him of it—he'd had to leave his car there—something wrong——" he explained. Marshall had interrupted then, lurching out of the kitchen with the gin bottle in his hand, full of an abounding though temporary good fellowship.

"Oh it's Mr. Yorke, is it? Come in, sir. Come in."

And Yorke had come in, and had drunk with Marshall and had sat watching her, whether she moved or sat still, almost as silently and quite as appraisingly as a farmer buying a heifer, but with something in his eyes and his half smile that might have been either admiration or derision.

Mrs. Marshall was beginning to grow resentful under the scrutiny when Marshall got up and went out of the room to fetch a fresh bottle. "Keep the cold out," he said——

Yorke leaned over the table then and spoke to her:

"I saw Philipson's portrait of you. I should like to dress you——" he paused, smiled at her flush, and added—"in Paris." After that Mrs. Marshall knew that she must have been mistaken about derision, and she let her eyes answer his.

When he got up to leave she went with him into the dark passage to open the door—Marshall wasn't safe on his legs by this time. And she had stumbled against him as if by accident. She called herself a fool now for doing it, but at the time it had been breathlessly, giddily exciting. If there had been any doubt in her mind as to whether she had misunderstood his steady contemplation of her, the promptitude and purpose with which he put his arm round her removed it. It was thrilling, with old Marshall sitting boozing a few feet away. When she had shut the door on Yorke she had waited a moment in the dark so that she could stop smiling—a triumphant, uncontrollable smile, because, for all he was "such a swank," as she put it to herself, he was "on."

She would not have been so triumphant if she had known Yorke's thoughts as he went through the farmyard to the short cut which had served as his excuse to "take a look at the skirt that Philipson has picked up." She would not, for one thing, have in the least understood his thoughts, for they were complex.

After his first reaction of excitement: "That handsome slut is ready for some fun," Yorke had proceeded to disguise the naked impulse to see that she had it, in garments of his own intellectual sophistication. He had, he reminded himself, taken up this chicken farm idea partly in order to get experience of what he summed up as "things in the raw." And what more raw could he find than this slatternly farmer's wife, beautiful, but in a way so veiled and strange that it took an artist's eye to see it. Doubtless, thought Yorke, Marshall and all the men she came across thought her a plain woman; for all her readiness with him, her tactics had been clumsy, not by any means those of a practised flirt; there was something crudely simple—yes, he said to himself, almost savage about them.

That pleased him. He realized that this would be just the sort of experience which should fertilize his mind for artistic creation. It began to seem to him that it was positively his duty to have an affair with Mrs. Marshall, an affair brutal, cruel, and sordid in the style of the most ruthless of the moderns.

So, brutal, cruel and sordid the thing had been from start to finish, leaving nothing now behind it but a silt of fear and hate. As she leaned by the attic window, her hands very cold yet damp with sweat, Mrs. Marshall found a name for Yorke that seemed to her worse than all the others. "Yes, he's a *gentleman!*" she thought, and the word summed up not only her own hatred, but the dumb resentment of many generations.

It was minutes before she moved away from the window and went downstairs. Her own breakfast things and Joe's were on the table. She began to gather them together, but slowly, because to wash up dishes in that stone sink in the corner of the scullery turned her stomach. She was always, even now, peering round in it for stains and splotches of blood. She had thought more than once of washing up in a tin basin in the kitchen—but then Joe might wonder why. She felt that he might even—somehow—guess.

She was carrying the dishes across the kitchen when she heard a footstep outside the window, and Sergeant Tucker went by.

His knock, as emphatic as the postman's, was blurred yet magnified by the noise of the blood in her ears. She put down the crockery hurriedly on a chair. She must not keep him waiting. Like Joe he might wonder why; he might guess; everything was like that now. She went to the door but it was as bad as moving in a dream when you must make haste to reach a place while all the time you were falling backwards.

"Good morning, ma'am," said Sergeant Tucker, "may I trouble you a moment?"

"Come in," said Mrs. Marshall and followed him into the kitchen.

Sergeant Tucker sat down in what had been Marshall's chair and looked round at the cheerless room. A domesticated man with a good wife, he was able to appreciate something at least of the dismal neglect of the place. There were gaps in the rows of plates on shelves of the dresser, and piles of plates in odd places about the room; on the window sill, on a chair, on the sewing machine. There was dust too everywhere, and though there was a fire in the grate it was a languid affair struggling for existence among a deep silt of yesterday's and the day before yesterday's cinders and dust. Mrs. Marshall

herself, her colourless hair carelessly scraped back, a smudge
of dust on her cheek, and a long ladder in one stocking, was
the most forlorn object there.

"I'm afraid this must be a very anxious time for you,
ma'am," said Sergeant Tucker.

"Yes," she whispered with some difficulty. If he had been
looking at her he would have thought her expression strange,
because, after her fears, she was astonished at such an opening.
But his kindly soul bade him turn his eyes away.

She had been standing. Now she took a chair and sat down
by the table with her hands on her lap and hidden under the
red woollen tablecloth.

"What do you want?" she said.

What Sergeant Tucker really wanted was to know where
Marshall was, alive or dead; and if dead, that his death had
been brought about by natural causes. Twenty years ago
Tucker had craved for that distinction in his profession which
can come only through successful participation in some case
of more than ordinary obscurity and violence. He would in
those days have welcomed the existence of far more highly
developed criminal tendencies in the population of Benmarsh than those village Cromwells possessed. By this time
however, these aspirations and yearnings had died down.
Tucker wanted a quiet life; though he was still intelligently
interested in criminal cases elsewhere, he did not desire their
occurrence in his own orbit.

He was therefore most unwilling to consider this disappearance of an elderly farmer as a possible case of crime; his unwillingness was increased by the fact that if a crime, it was,
as it were, Peppard's property. But, though Tucker's desires,
and his reason alike, repelled the idea of murder, Peppard's
confidence and conviction were beginning to tell. The Sergeant, though reluctantly, had begun to feel that perhaps he
ought at least to consider the hypothesis.

All the way up Oldners Lane he had been rehearsing how
best to introduce this sinister idea to Mrs. Marshall. He did
not want—above all things he did not want a scene. He must
therefore proceed with caution. He began, with just that arti-

ficiality of tone which comes from the use of pre-considered words.

"Well, ma'am. I'm afraid we've no news of your good husband. No one of his description reported. So we must consider other eventualities. In fact something quite different from what we suppose may have happened to him."

There was a loud and sudden clatter. Even Tucker glanced round quickly, but Mrs. Marshall fairly jumped out of her chair. A piece of coal, falling on the hearth, had disturbed the balance of a long and heavy steel poker, with a rusty knob as big as a small apple, and the poker had brought down with it a pair of tongs of the same proportions.

"Now! Now!" said Tucker soothingly, as he got up and put the fire irons back in their place. The poor thing's nerves, he thought, were all to bits. She sat down again, but he saw her fingers twitch. He waited, hoping that at least she would ask him what he had been hinting at, and thus give him, as it were, a take-off. But she did not raise her eyes and she said nothing.

"Well, ma'am," Sergeant Tucker's cheery voice sank to the most sympathetic and reassuring murmur he was capable of, "well, ma'am, we hope it wasn't foul play, but then again, if it was, the sooner we look facts in the face the better. What I want to know from you is whether your husband had any— whether you know any one that had a grudge against him. Take your time now. Think!"

Mrs. Marshall was thinking. She had been thinking for several days. Mr. Yorke had told her—in spite of all their intimacy he was always "Mr. Yorke" to her—that she must say nothing, know nothing, do nothing. He had told her that he would "fix it up so that no one would think it was murder." And that tomorrow he would see that Marshall went to the bottom of Pilly's Pond, and then they would be quite safe.

But in two directions this programme had gone wrong. Marshall was still—where they had put him. And Peppard and Mrs. Peppard were saying that it was murder. "Oh! your poor dear 'usband, Mrs. Marshall. Oh! you poor creature—— An 'orrible bloody murder, Peppard says."

Mrs. Marshall therefore, hemmed in on every side, scared and desperate, and remembering always that "they hang women in England, you know," had decided that if Tucker came again she must say something, in place of the nothing that Yorke had ordered. And now Tucker's question opened the way, providentially it seemed, for just that invention which she had laboriously devised. She would disobey Mr. Yorke. But she would be very careful.

"I dunno," she said slowly, "I dunno of any as—— Not properly—— But——"

"Well." Sergeant Tucker sat very still so as not to frighten his bird. He listened.

"Well there was a man here——"

"When?"

"That afternoon."

"Now then," said Sergeant Tucker taken between wind and water by this startling news. "Why didn't you tell us before?"

Mrs. Marshall raised her eyes, those pale, strangely beautiful eyes that Philipson had admired, and Yorke had called "thief's eyes." She gripped her fingers together under the table and wished to goodness she hadn't ventured on this flight of imagination.

"I don't know. I was—— I didn't think. You said——"

Sergeant Tucker remembered with misgiving and self-reproach his determination that this should be a case of disappearance only. How that man Peppard would crow!

"Well! Tell us now," he said with some asperity. "Had he ever been here before?"

Mrs. Marshall thought not. No—not as she remembered for sure.

"Well, what was he like?"

Mrs. Marshall didn't seem able to say. He wasn't tall, nor short, he wasn't a young man, nor was he old, even middle-aged didn't exactly fit him it seemed, the best word was "middlin'."

"Was he clean shaven?"

Mrs. Marshall hadn't seen him close enough to know—not for sure.

"Where was he then?"

"In the field with Marshall."

"And where were you?"

"Up in the bedroom—— Like I told you."

"What sort of clothes did he wear?"

Mrs. Marshall had to be prompted. She apparently had forgotten the component parts of a man's wardrobe.

"Hat?"

"No—it was a cap."

"Overcoat?"

"No."

"Coat. What colour?"

"Oh just—just dirty colour. Like men wear."

"Trousers like the coat?"

"No. Grey," she thought, "or perhaps—— I dunno."

"Well," said the Sergeant with commendable patience, "what were they doing in the field? Were they quarrelling?"

"I couldn't say for sure. I were too far off. But it looked like it."

"And did your husband and the man go off together?"

"Ye-es."

"Which way? Towards the Mallingford road—— Green Lane way?" Tucker jerked his head in the direction towards which the attic window looked.

"No," said Mrs. Marshall, quite positive this time. "No, the other way." She pointed up Footpad Hill. "You can't see Green Lane way from the bedrooms."

Sergeant Tucker was grateful for firm ground under his feet. In so much that was doubtful this then was sure. The woman, he felt, was talking about something she'd seen.

"And Marshall didn't come back here after?"

"No."

"And what time was it that you saw this man with Marshall?"

But Mrs. Marshall was no more help. It was after dinner— quite a while. But not tea time—oh no—it wasn't as late as

that not by a long way. Pressed to choose between two or three
o'clock, "only roughly you know," she thought it was probably
two; or perhaps half-past; or it might have been a bit later because time does fly so.

Sergeant Tucker gathered himself together and stood up.

"This looks as if it might be a bad business, I'm afraid," he
said on his way to the door.

Mrs. Marshall came after him. In the doorway she stopped
and pointed towards the stacks and the dangling black corpses
of marauding rooks.

"They went up that way. I know they didn't come back because I was on the lookout for Marshall."

"I see," said Tucker. He was frowning. Mrs. Marshall had
pointed in the direction of Ipsden woods.

15

POISON IS A SURE WAY

IT WAS AS he was drinking his third cup of tea that Yorke thought of a way of killing Philipson. He drank the tea off hastily, finished the sandwich on his plate, and went up to his room. The job would need thinking out. And there should be no mistake this time.

Upstairs, having shut the door carefully, he crossed the room to the little cupboard beside the fireplace. He was, though he did not know it, treading softly, and avoiding, as much as possible, the bare boards of the floor between the rugs. When he had opened the cupboard he stood for quite a long time staring at the shelves. They contained his pharmacy, which, like all his belongings, was arranged and maintained with exact care. The bottles, small and large, stood in orderly battalions. They were of very varied contents, for Yorke was a man who disliked throwing anything away.

The top shelf was high up, a long stretch even for so tall a man as Yorke. To see what was on it he stepped back a few paces, and stood staring up for quite a long time. Right at the back of the shelf, so that he could only see it by craning his neck, was a packet, wrapped in the chemist's immaculate white paper. Mr. Yorke reached up, pushed aside the bottles

in front, and lifted down the packet. Half had been used, but
the flap of the parcel had been tucked in, and an indiarubber
band held all in place. "Potassium cyanide. Poison. Not to
be taken," was printed on the label. "Lucky I got the powder,"
Mr. Yorke said to himself, "Saves a bit of trouble." He put it
down on the end of the chest of drawers.

The next thing was to find the bottle of sulphonal that he'd
kept since the time that he'd had a gastric ulcer, nearly a year
ago. The bottle was almost empty, but even now it gave him
a twinge of regret to empty the powder out into his palm
and tip that through the open window into the snow upon the
sill.

He came back to the shelves with the empty bottle in his
hand, and took up the white packet. But for a long moment
he stood still, listening. Suppose any one should come upstairs, knock on his door, open it, and see him doing this?
The thought ran like cold water down his spine. And it was
not only that he feared to be seen. His face, even his mouth,
felt cold. It was an awful thing to do.

Poison. A poisoner. He remembered how he and the Veres's
had been talking last summer about a poisoning case. He
could remember the creeping shiver that had gone through
his mind as he imagined the poisoner—it was a woman—
getting ready her husband's food, with one eye on the door
and every nerve at a strain, as she listened, then quickly tipped
the deadly stuff into the pan. Now he was doing it. He
muttered the words through his teeth—"Now I'm doing it"
—because unless he said them aloud he could not believe it.

A sudden scream and a shout outside sent the blood with a
shock up to his throat and head. His heart started to pound.
Even when he realized that the noise was made only by some
larking boys in the lane, it still thumped in his chest as if it
were a hand hammering on a door. He ceased to find strange
that on which he was engaged, and remembered only the
thing in the field, and Philipson who might, at any moment,
remember.

He took off the rubber band from the packet, and poured
half of the powder into the bottle, refolded the flap of the

packet, corked the bottle and set both down. It pleased him that he had not spilt any of the powder. "I did that well," he told himself, and felt confidence warm him with a glow.

Now he must arrange things. The bottle which had held the sulphonal he pushed right to the back of the shelf where the packet had stood. The packet itself he stood in front of it, and moved up a small supporting force of bottles. Then he shut the doors. Everything was ready.

After dinner, a dinner of which Philipson, sitting very glum and drooping, hardly ate at all, the two men went back to the sitting room as usual. Yorke took out his pipe. He told himself that he would smoke half of it before he spoke. Smoking would steady him. But he could not wait so long. As he lit it he looked across at Philipson through the puffs of smoke and above the little dragged flame of the match. He threw the match away, took deep pulls, and spoke.

"Feeling any better?"

"No—— Thanks."

"I'm sorry about that." Yorke made a long arm, poured out his coffee and stared into the dark steaming liquid.

"I say, Philipson——"

"Yes."

"Are you sleeping all right?"

Philipson gave a sudden crackling laugh which seemed to startle himself, for he shut his mouth on it. After a second he said: "What do you think? No. Damnably."

"Tckh! That's bad." Yorke's voice was all that was sympathetic. "Are you taking anything to make you sleep?"

Philipson did not answer that question. Instead he jumped up out of his chair, took two strides towards the window, then stopped short, as if he did not know why he had started off that way.

"Look here, Yorke—— What am I going to do?" He beat his hands together. "What am I——?"

Yorke interrupted him quickly——

"Never mind that now. What you want is a good night's

sleep. I can see that your nerves are all to pieces. We'll talk over what we'd better do in the morning."

Philipson came back to his chair and flopped into it again. He looked as if he had been scolded and hadn't any justification to give.

"*Have* you been taking anything?" Yorke asked again.

"Aspirin," said Philipson briefly and remembered with confusion the trouble there had been on the night he had bought the aspirin. Yorke remembered it too and was glad that Philipson had reminded him of it.

"You see," Philipson turned to him, anxious to cover up the recollection, "I get off to sleep for a bit and then I wake up." His voice appealed for help.

"Damn the fellow!" Yorke said to himself.

"Have you ever tried sulphonal?" he said to Philipson.

Philipson hadn't.

"They gave it me when I had my ulcer, you know. It's a good deal stronger than aspirin. I've got some left and I'll give you a dose tonight if you like."

"Isn't it——" Philipson began, and stopped. "Isn't it," he said in a peculiar tone, "the kind of thing that—I mean, can you do yourself in by taking an overdose?"

Yorke laughed loudly because, taken aback as he was, he could think of nothing to say for a moment. Could Philipson possibly suspect—something? He must be careful, very careful. But at least compunction had ceased to incommode him.

"Not unless you took a pound or so," he said and laughed again. "I haven't got that much."

Philipson nodded vaguely.

"Will you try it?" Yorke asked him, keeping his voice under control.

"Well—— Thanks very much," said Philipson, as if he did not much care what he did.

"I think you'll find it will do the trick," Yorke heard himself say. "I don't think you'll wake up after this." He did not know what had driven him to risk that colossal bit of impudence. He raised his coffee cup and drank hastily; if he had not, he thought he would have let out a silly shrill giggle.

To Yorke's great relief, it was still early when Philipson got up and said he was going to bed.

Yorke got up too. "Well, get yourself a good tot of whiskey, and I'll come up with you and find you that sulphonal."

Philipson mumbled some sort of apology for being a nuisance. Yorke told him, angrily, to shut up. He waited at the foot of the stairs till Philipson came out with his whiskey, then they went up, Yorke going first.

Philipson would have stopped at his bedroom door.

But—— "I've got it somewhere in my room," said Yorke. "Come on," and opened the door. Philipson came on.

Yorke ran his fingers along the front top shelf, ticking off as it were one bottle after another; iodine, witch hazel, peroxide of hydrogen, boracic lotion.

"Where the devil is it? Must have got behind," he muttered.

He reached up and took down the iodine: "Here—take this."

Philipson took it. Yorke's hand came down with the boracic powder. Philipson took that too, and the bottle of witch hazel.

"No—it's not there," Yorke grumbled. He reached up again. This time he lifted down a white chemist's packet. He turned. "Can you hold that?"

"Wait a minute!" Philipson hastily set the other bottles down on the chest of drawers, and took the packet.

"Ah!" said Yorke. "Here it is."

He brought his hand down, and dangled the bottle in front of Philipson's face, the label towards him.

"Now," said Yorke. "Where's your whiskey?"

Philipson put down the packet of poison with the bottles and held out his tumbler. Yorke had ready the medicinal spoon he always kept in the cupboard. He measured out a dose of the powder, and dropped it into the topaz coloured whiskey.

It settled to the bottom and stayed there, a layer of white sediment.

He was glad that Philipson was watching the stuff in the tumbler, because he knew then what it meant when people said—"his jaw dropped." He saw for a moment his whole plan wrecked. But his mind worked quickly. "I'd forgotten," he muttered, "it takes a hell of a long time to dissolve. Look here. I'll stir it for you. You go and get into bed and I'll bring it to you."

He turned away. Philipson had to put down the tumbler on the chest of drawers; then he went off, mumbling apologetic thanks.

The next minutes were anxious ones for Yorke. But after a lot of passionate stirring the stuff did dissolve. He wound his handkerchief loosely round the glass—there must be no finger-prints of his on it—took it along to Philipson's room, knocked and went in. Philipson sat in bed, his knees drawn up to his chin.

"Sorry! The glass may be a bit wet. I spilt some." Yorke held it out at the full stretch of his arm. He tried to avoid the touch of Philipson's fingers, but could not quite. They were very hot. The thought jumped in his mind—"They'll be cold soon." He backed away from the bed.

"Now then," he said, and because he was afraid of what his voice might do, he spoke loudly and with jocularity. "Now then, drink it up like a good boy."

Philipson still held it. He sniffed at it, but without much hope of smelling anything through his cold.

"Is it very beastly?" he asked plaintively.

"No of course not. Hold your nose. It'll be down in a minute. Come along now." Yorke did not realize how absurdly the scene resembled that of an overdriven, distracted mother wrestling with a rebellious child over a dose of medicine.

Then he swore aloud. The telephone was ringing downstairs. He heard Mrs. Harker's chair in the kitchen below scrape along the tiles as she pushed it back. He couldn't have Mrs. Harker coming out into the hall and hearing him leave Mr. Philipson's room.

He hung on his heel a moment.

"I must go." He was at the door, then on the landing. He looked back. Philipson had raised the glass to his lips, his nose was pinched between two fingers; he looked grotesquely comic.

A sudden overwhelming desire to laugh, to laugh, to scream

with laughter, caught hold of Yorke. He crammed his handkerchief into his mouth as he made for the stairs.

For the next half hour he sat by the fire, with a book on his
knee, but he did not read. He listened. He heard Agnes let
herself out of the back door. He heard Mrs. Harker go upstairs
to bed. But what must by now have happened in Philipson's
room seemed to have passed in the complete, indifferent silence of night.

At last he got up, and went over to Philipson's desk. He was
glad to be doing something, though what he had to do would
be, he knew, very difficult.

It was. After a dozen attempts to write even a couple of
lines in Philipson's hand—a hand which in its flowing nicety
was in strange contrast with the untidy little man himself,
Yorke gave up in despair, bundled together all his practice
attempts, and rammed them savagely into the fire. He would
have to do without a confession of guilt. After all, he comforted himself, the suicide itself would be the most convincing, though tacit confession.

Yet, as the paper charred to black fluttering rags in the fire,
he stood pinching up his lips with his fingers, because something was needed, something which would make it quite clear
that Philipson had committed suicide. Then he jerked up his
chin. He went over to the bookcase. His hand lingered over
one shelf, descended to another. Yes. There it was. He took
out a slim small volume—*A Shropshire Lad*—opened it, and
turned over the pages.

> "Shot? so quick, so clean an ending?
>   Oh that was right, lad, that was brave:
>   Yours was not an ill for mending,
>   'Twas best to take it to the grave.
>
>   Oh you had forethought, you could reason
>   And saw your road and where it led,
>   And early wise and brave in season
>   Put the pistol to your head.

Oh soon, and better so than later
    After long disgrace and scorn,
You shot dead the household traitor,
    The soul that should not have been born."

That would do. It was neater, and far safer than a forged letter, and the police would not know that Philipson would never have thought of such a subtle way of saying good bye to the world. Yorke smiled suddenly, a peculiar smile. He took a pencil out of his pocket, and scored two heavy lines on the page beside the verse, and, though with compunction, turned down a big dog's ear at the corner.

"That's more like him," he murmured; "Philipson always is—always was," he corrected himself with something like an inward giggle, "a heathen with books."

Going upstairs he was careful to make an ordinary amount of noise, lest Mrs. Harker should still be awake. He even hummed a song, but softly, because he did not want to waken her. In his own room the cluster of bottles still stood where Philipson had put them down. The police, finding them there, would find Philipson's fingerprints on them. The packet of potassium cyanide was beside them. Yorke picked it up in his handkerchief and slipped it into his pocket. He hoped he had not blurred the fingerprints on it.

Philipson's door was beyond his. He stepped quietly out upon the passage, and laid his hand on the knob. The whole world was quiet, quiet as death. But in a minute he would have to break the quiet with a shout; "Mrs. Harker! Mrs. Harker! Come here! Something is wrong with Mr. Philipson!" He felt for a second that he would never be able to do it, that he had lost the power of speech and of movement too, that he would stand holding the knob of the door, and unable to turn it, till Mrs. Harker woke up and found him there—the poisoner, going into the dead man's room.

Some contraction of his hand there must have been. He found the door opening; he pushed it wider, and stood on the threshold.

"Philipson!" he whispered.

The bed creaked. There was a grunt, and then a peevish: "Hullo! What the hell is it!"

Yorke stood there and said nothing. In the half darkness of the room he could see the bedclothes violently agitated, then Philipson's face poked itself up.

"What is it?"

Yorke pulled himself together with a jerk.

"Sorry. I wanted to see if you'd got to sleep."

"Well, I had, and now you've wakened me up, and God knows when I'll get off again."

"I'm sorry. Didn't you take that stuff?" It took Yorke all his strength to keep his voice light and steady over that.

"No, I didn't. I had to put it down to sneeze and I put it down on the edge of the table, and it fell off."

"Oh," said Yorke. "Well, I'll get you some more."

Philipson, who had been peering at him above the bed-clothes, flopped down now and turned over on his side. "No thanks," he said. "I took a heap of aspirin and I don't want to be sick."

Yorke shut the door and went to his own room. The feelings of a murderer he had known already; now he knew the feelings of a man who has failed to commit murder. They were extremely painful, being compounded of cold fear, a feeling of sickness, and a burning, futile rage.

16

PHILIPSON DECIDES
TO MAKE AN END

O N THAT SUNDAY morning it was clear that there
was soon to be a change in the weather. The snow
was still there, the sun shone, but across the blue heaven,
chased by a light wind, flew filmy rags of cloud, that were as
yet little more than shining mist. Nor was the snow silence
complete as it had been. Very softly, as in an undertone, hidden waters had begun to converse together. When Mr. Yorke
looked out, something near the window was dripping, not
fast, but regularly, and there came a sound like a whispered
"shish" as a lump of snow slid down the roof into the garden
below. If the thaw really set in the snow would be gone before
evening, so slight had the fall been. And if the snow was gone
—Yorke stuck his head out of the window and stared eagerly
up into the sky—Old Marshall should go into Pilly's Ponds.

And Philipson too. Yorke had made up his mind during
the night in which he had had little more sleep than the man
next door to him. He would ask Philipson to come out in the
car after dinner, then a blow with a spanner, and two weighted
sacks instead of one in the Ponds. And then, for Yorke, a quick
get-away.

He managed to avoid having breakfast with Philipson. He

did his best to avoid him during the morning. But he failed.
Philipson cornered him in the old cow shippen where now the
chicken meal was stored. He came to the door and stood there
peering into the shadowy interior. Yorke did not move, but
Philipson saw him.

"I say, Yorke."

"What is it?" Yorke's tone was discouraging.

Philipson did not speak again till he stood beside the bin
out of which Yorke was dipping meal. Then he said:

"I've been thinking."

Yorke dropped the scoop, dusted his hands, and slipped one
into his pocket to get hold of the thing that he had carried
there for the last few days.

"Well?"

"If I were to go to Tucker——" said Philipson and stopped
and looked aside. Yorke had the pistol half out of his pocket
when he went on: "And tell him, he'd——he'd have me certified."

"Tell him what? What do you mean?"

Philipson said with difficulty: "Well you see——if I killed
Marshall——I must have been——mad."

As if, the word once out, an impediment to speech was removed, he went on talking fast, more than half to himself, and
all the time straining one hand against the other as if he were
trying to strip off a pair of tight gloves.

"I know what happens when someone's certified. We had
an old maid when I was a boy, and she went——she——she went
like me. She thought the Holy Ghost was flying about the
room and she was afraid of him settling on her cap. We
thought it awfully funny when mother told us. And dad sent
the other maid for the doctor, and he came——it was Sunday
morning, but we hadn't gone to church——we thought it was
all great fun. I remember we were all at the window, we kids,
watching the cab——it was a cab then of course——because we'd
seen the policeman sitting inside. And then the doctor came
out with his hand on the old thing's arm, and she tried to
break back to the house. We didn't like that much; my sister
cried. But the Bobby got out and they got her into the cab

somehow and then it bowled off. I never thought till—till last week, what she was feeling like as they drove. But I'm thinking of it all the time now."

Yorke, half listening to all this silly and irrelevant stuff, was debating in his mind if it were possible after all to have Philipson certified. If it were, then whether he remembered or no, his witness would be invalid. But what story to tell without coming far too near the truth? He wished to goodness the fool would stop talking—Sunday morning church, cabs, all the rest, what did it matter when Yorke had to decide and decide quickly?

"Perhaps," Philipson went on, "perhaps if I hadn't been in that shell-shock hospital I wouldn't have funked it. But the noises you used to hear—fellows crying, and laughing sometimes, and when you met any one in the passages you didn't look at him, you didn't want to. You were always afraid of something—too afraid to run away. And you felt that perhaps if you had been the only—the only cracked one among sane people you might have been able to get better, but all the other fellows—you can't get your mind back. It's buried —under the weight."

The monologue ceased. Yorke was thankful; he hardly noticed when Philipson said, still gently, but in a firmer voice: "So I can't bear it."

Yorke could not make a plan. All that he thought of was impossible. His mind was like a dancing mouse going round and round. "This strain," he thought, "it's too much. I'll have to shoot him, or club him on the head and take the chance. I can't think now." And the creature was talking again.

"And it's not only that I can't bear to be locked up—I—I can't bear to be—myself. I mean—— You see——" he floundered and then forced out: "They hang ordinary murderers. They wouldn't hang me. But if I shot myself——"

Yorke said nothing. He only stood staring.

Philipson said: "I wouldn't have told you, only I wanted to borrow your pistol, and I couldn't find it in the drawer when I looked for it."

Yorke was so amazed that he almost drew it out of his

pocket and said: "Here it is," but he recollected himself in time. Instead he stammered: "But why?—But when?"

Philipson hesitated a moment. Then he did not answer; he asked a question. "Did you mean me to—to do it when you left me with that pistol that other day? I thought afterwards that perhaps you did. I believe I should have done, if the thing hadn't been empty. I sat there thinking about it, but I suppose I hadn't quite made up my mind enough to put in a cartridge. But it would have been so easy if only there had been a round in it."

Yorke, for the first time in his life, thought scorn of subtlety.

"You want to shoot yourself?" he asked stupidly.

Philipson nodded. "I think I ought to. Don't you?"

Yorke could not avoid meeting his eyes, and then could not look away. He knew that Philipson would believe whatever he said; he had only to speak to condemn him, as surely as any judge in scarlet, to death. He said at last:

"I'm afraid you—ought to."

Philipson said nothing for quite a time. Then:

"Thank you. You'll lend me a pistol?"

Yorke said that he would.

To have come to a decision composes the mind; in a sense it even cancels the circumstances which conditioned it. As soon as Philipson had determined that he would kill himself, the torturing questions of the last days ceased in a sudden quiet. He might be a murderer, but he would not be that or anything else much longer. He sat through lunch in a sort of daze, eating little and talking hardly at all. When they went back to the sitting room he found himself inclined, by the mere comfort of peace in his brain, to stretch out his feet to the fire and go to sleep. A little spring, not of hope, because he did not consciously look forward, but of zest for life, began to run down below his mind. It was with a dull shock that he realized the futility of it. Things were only better, and peace conceivable, because he was going to step out of life into the nothing that he expected, without being able, any more than any other human being, to conceive of the absolute negative.

The small shock unsettled him. He was not afraid of dying, at least he thought not, but he began to worry about a number of subsidiary matters. When should he do it? Where? Would he be able to shoot so straight that he would be dead before any one found him. He thought with horror of people staring at him as he lay dying.

Yorke startled him by getting up abruptly. "You'll have letters you want to write," he said curtly. "I suppose you've made your will?"

Philipson did not mind the curtness. He thought: "This is beastly for Yorke, sitting about with a man who's going to kill himself."

Yorke said: "I'll see to things outside," and went out. "I shan't be back for a bit," he shouted through the shut door.

But had he letters to write? Philipson considered the suggestion when Yorke had gone past the window, head down, with his quick thrusting stride. He hadn't any family left nearer than cousins, and he could see no point at all in sitting down and writing:

"Dear Ted,
I am going to kill myself tonight——"

But there was one letter he wanted to write; and he must not write it. He wanted to write to the Vicar. He got up and went towards his desk. He said to himself that he owed it to Tellwright to explain; that it would be a rotten thing to let him hear it, and hear it all wrong from gossips in the village. But, with the writing pad in his hand he knew he couldn't do it, because what was really in his mind was that the Vicar would send the letter to Justina—so that she should understand.

His hand went out again to the pad that he had put back. He was assailed by a strong desire to write direct to Justina. If he could do that, he thought, he wouldn't mind anything. Then he chucked the pad down, and when it tipped off the edge of the desk and fell to the ground, he kicked it underneath. His mind was not clear, but something that was partly pride and partly scrupulousness forbade him to satisfy the desire. If he put it into words at all the words were bald:

"I've no business to."

But the thought of the two Tellwrights—he resolutely made it two—upset his precarious peace of mind. He began to wander about the room, dogged by a distress that increased till he could not be sure if his chest really ached or if he were only miserable. It was while he stood absently prodding with his finger the bulb of a half-opened hyacinth of a sleepy, sultry blue which stood in the window ledge, that understanding came into his mind, and he said, almost aloud:

"I suppose I really care for her quite a lot."

As if the enlightenment told him what to do, he went quickly over to his desk, searched about till he found crayon and brown paper, and then, rapidly and surely, but without haste, for he had forgotten time, he began to sketch a likeness of Justina Tellwright.

Just at tea-time—he had timed himself carefully—Yorke came along the path as he had come last Tuesday, and as last Tuesday, paused and looked in through the sitting room window. Opposite him, crouched over his drawing board, sat Philipson, his finger ends white with chalk, a smudge of dusty white across his cheek. As Yorke stared in he looked up, turned painfully red, hurriedly unpinned the drawing, and shoved it into his desk.

Yorke came slowly to the door. He did not care a tinker's curse what it was that Philipson was drawing. The trouble was that he should be in a state to draw anything at all. Hadn't he given the fellow time enough? he thought. A doubt, piercing and disabling, struck him. Had Philipson changed his mind. Was it all still to do?

He stood for a moment dangling the key ring from his finger before he opened the door. All round the garden the snow was coarsening and thinning away. In some places the earth showed through, wet and very black; where the slot of the hunting cat had pitted the snow for the past days was a trail of little green smudges. The sun was hidden by brownish vaporous clouds. The air was thickening already, as if dusk were already come; it would be dark early, and probably by then the fog would have come down.

He lingered on the doorstep even when he had opened the door, looking back upon the heavy dying of the day. If Philipson had changed his mind, Yorke knew that he must be prepared for that struggle in the car, and flight after. And his brain was very tired of planning. He could have wept with pity for himself.

Tea was a constrained meal. Yorke was calculating chances, imagining, trying to prepare for all possible contingencies. Philipson was suffering, not only from the dead pressure of mental exhaustion, but also from a trivial but distressing embarrassment. He was perfectly aware that Yorke had not expected to find him alive; he felt like a guest who has outstayed his welcome, and yet he did not know how to explain why he had not already taken himself off. It seemed crude, even to him, to say, with a teacup in one hand, that he wanted to shoot himself somewhere that would be perfectly private, and that therefore he must wait for dark. He had decided that he could not do it in the house because of the trouble and mess that it would make for Mrs. Harker. But you simply couldn't, he felt, explain all that. Yet, if he did not somehow manage to bring the conversation round to that topic, how could he ask for Yorke's pistol. And it was now nearly dark outside. The silence between them grew so oppressive that he could not think of anything to break it.

When Mrs. Harker had taken away the tray Yorke got up abruptly, and went out of the room. He came back several minutes later and laid something on the arm of Philipson's chair.

Philipson put his hand down on it. It was very cold, and a sharp thrill ran up to his brain and set his hair pricking. He felt his heart bump heavily several times. He slipped the pistol into his pocket and got up.

"Thanks very much," he said to Yorke's back, and got no answer but a grunt.

After the discomfort of his heart had quieted Philipson felt a certain relief. It was so simple. He hadn't had to say anything. He need not even say good-bye. He went over to the door, walking lightly and a little giddily.

"So long," he said, and went into the hall.

17

THE VICAR DOESN'T BELIEVE IT

ABOUT SIX MINUTES before Philipson shut the garden gate behind him, Mr. Tellwright was hanging up his surplice in the vestry of Benmarsh church. The choir and the churchwardens had gone; his only company was a recumbent Elizabethan gentlewoman in a thick stone ruff. The Vicar hung up his surplice, and stroked down the folds, yet still seemed to be interested in the texture of the linen. Actually his thoughts were on quite another matter. He had decided, or rather he had almost decided, though against his will, that it is sometimes the duty of a Christian and a priest to do what he much disliked—that is to butt in. There was a gleam of amusement in his mind at what would have been Justina's phrase, but the thought of Justina quenched the gleam. What Mr. Tellwright was trying to make himself do, was to go to Philipson and force his confidence.

His decision—he knew it all along—was never in doubt. He only needed time to beat down his own unwillingness to intrude upon another man's privacy of mind. When he had left the vestry and ground the great old key round in the lock, he turned along the dark flank of the church towards the road, instead of across the graveyard to the Vicarage. And he found, once he had started, that he was eaten up with impatience to reach Miller's Green. It was not the impatience of a man who wants to get a difficult thing over and done with; it was an inexplicable sense of hurry and urgency.

But it was very difficult to be quick in the dark, especially with the snow melting under foot, and this unseasonable fog. Now that the brightness of the snow had passed, there was nothing to lighten the impenetrable obscurity of the night, and the road was very slippery. He began to wish that he had gone back to the Vicarage to fetch his stick, and an electric torch. But, though he might have turned back for them, and even thought of doing so, he would not, because he felt he could not spare the time.

If it had been a clear night he would have saved himself a few minutes by cutting across the fields, past a little wood where lovers were always to be found on summer evenings, and over a brook. But tonight short cuts were impossible. He crossed the main road by the A.A. box, and took the smaller road that led to Miller's Green, and, after many windings, to Mallingford.

When he had been walking for a few minutes he could not tell, well as he knew every lane and path round Benmarsh, just how far he had come. There was a group of cottages mid-way along the road to Miller's Green but, though he strained his eyes, he could catch no glimmer of light from their windows. Then his foot touched a loose stone, he stumbled on another, and pulled up. He had almost fallen, but at least he knew where he was. The County Council had lately dumped a pile of stones for road mending beside the stile into the fields.

It was just then, as he stood still, that he heard the sound of footsteps coming down the lane towards him, and saw a faint, swinging blur of light. It was someone walking with a flash lamp.

The Vicar moved forward and stopped, for the light had gone out. Whoever carried it had stopped too. Mr. Tellwright, promptly rejecting any sinister suggestion, decided that it must be some nervous female parishioner.

"It's all right," he said. "It's only the Vicar."

There was no answer.

Mr. Tellwright moved forward, but he could not help wishing that he had brought his stick. Then someone spoke.

"I wanted to write to you." It was Philipson's voice. "But I didn't want to see you."

Mr. Tellwright, shaken by the suddenness and strangeness with which he had met the man he had gone out to find, spoke more abruptly than was his wont. "What are you talking about?"

Philipson did not answer. The Vicar's heart almost failed him. It was true then, not only what Peppard had said but what he himself had feared when he found Philipson at Miller's Green yesterday with a pistol in his hand. In the heavy darkness he felt that he was powerless to help or prevent. But he persisted.

"Where are you going?"

"Into the fields—just here."

Mr. Tellwright knew that Philipson turned his face towards the stile. His dread of this interview had passed; so had his feeling of impotence. He had been urged to hasten upon a mission, and he knew now why he had been sent, and in haste. But still, he would have the answer from Philipson's own mouth.

"What for?" he asked, and waited.

"Look here," Philipson began at last, in a tone strangely like that of a boy labouring to excuse himself to a schoolmaster—"I wanted to write to you—I did—— Only—I—I——" he floundered, "I really couldn't. But I can't help it—I must—I can't go on. I can't go on, going about the world, having killed a man, when I might—you see—again."

Mr. Tellwright was smitten by the full force of reality, so incomparably more potent than any fear. It was true. Philipson had said it.

"You have killed a man," he said.

"Oh hush!" came Philipson's voice out of the dark.

"And now you intend to kill yourself?"

"Yes—I——"

Mr. Tellwright stepped close to him and laid one hand on his right wrist.

"Do you not realize that it is my duty, both as a priest and a citizen, to do my best to prevent you?"

"Oh dear, I hadn't thought of that." Philipson spoke with such blank simplicity that Mr. Tellwright would have laughed if it had been any laughing matter.

"And I will try to prevent you," said Mr. Tellwright his hand still on Philipson's. "Even to using force if necessary. I am an old man, but I would do my best. I don't think you would like that."

Philipson, picturing a rough and tumble with the Vicar in the dark road, replied that—no, he would not like it. He did not even try to free his wrist but stood quite still, utterly at a loss before this new difficulty.

A few minutes ago he had been plodding along, almost as vacant as a sleep walker, all things settled and determined; no more need for thought; only one thing to do, and that would be done by a simple pressure of his thumb. And now the Vicar had got in the way, and he hadn't the least idea what to do next.

He said again: "Oh dear!" and then, "do let me go!"

But Mr. Tellwright still held him by the wrist, and suddenly the grasp tightened. Someone was coming along the lane on a bicycle. There was nothing to be seen yet, but they heard a ping, ping. The sound came nearer and was repeated —ping, ping, ping.

Mr. Tellwright said, instinctively raising his voice:

"Look out!"

The ping ping and a blurred light came at them in the obscurity, a shape went slowly by with a long swishing noise of wheels in the wet snow.

"Good night!" came Sergeant Tucker's deep voice.

"Good night!" Mr. Tellwright answered. Philipson said nothing, but Mr. Tellwright felt him try to drag his hand free and then again stand very still.

As for Mr. Tellwright himself, he was, by his own choice, plunged into a dilemma. And the choice had been voluntary, not merely instinctive, for he was a man who, for all his gentle aloofness, could keep his presence of mind at a crisis. He had chosen not to stop the Sergeant, because Philipson—even if he had committed murder and intended suicide—was Philipson. But he knew he had done wrong.

"That was Tucker," he said, but the words meant more than that, and Philipson understood that they did.

He, also, knew that the Vicar ought to have stopped Tucker, and given him in charge, and the knowledge tore to shreds the dull smothering indifference that had possessed his mind. Once more he was aware of past and future; he was cornered and desperate. He must get away to the bare spinney where he could be alone, and—and do it. But he couldn't bear to force Mr. Tellwright's thin fingers from his wrist.

"I must," he cried, "I really must. You must let me. Madmen aren't like other people."

Mr. Tellwright did not know what Philipson was driving at.

"Marshall drank, but he was not mad," he said, the more sternly because of his own recent lapse from duty.

Philipson told him curtly: "I'm not talking about Marshall. I'm——" He stopped there as if he had run into a stone wall. If it had not been for the privacy of the fog which made himself and Mr. Tellwright like two disembodied, eyeless souls, talking to each other in the churchyard from their neighbouring graves, he could not have gone on.

But Mr. Tellwright had let go his wrist, and Philipson, backing away, hardly saw even the thickening in the fog which was the Vicar. He began to say something, and realized that certainly Mr. Tellwright could not hear that. He cleared his throat and said it again; but even so the only words he could make audible were——

"homicidal maniac."

They were however the heart of it, and having got that out he could say the rest.

When he had finished, no answer came for a pause that seemed endless.

Then the Vicar said:

"My dear fellow—— My dear fellow. I simply don't believe it."

"What?" asked Philipson stupidly. Of all possible things that Mr. Tellwright might have said, that was the last that he would have imagined.

"I simply don't believe it."

Philipson took a step forward. He bumped into the Vicar, mumbled an apology, and fetched up on the heap of stones. It made something to sit on, and he was thankful for it.

"If you don't mind," he said, "I'll sit down a minute."

"Yes, of course, do!" said Mr. Tellwright, and felt, with a fraction of his mind, that they were behaving ridiculously like two old ladies in a drawing room. "But it must be very wet," he added, going back to the days when he was bringing up Justina. "You'd better not sit too long."

Philipson gave a kind of giggle.

"It is wet, and damn' cold." He sat there for a few seconds and then Mr. Tellwright heard the stones roll under his feet as he got up.

"But I don't see," said Philipson, as though there had been no pause, "I don't see how—— It must be true. That bit of bone—the hairs——" His teeth chattered.

Mr. Tellwright shook his head, and then remembered that Philipson could not see.

"I don't believe it," he repeated stoutly. He felt that he was miserably inadequate to the occasion, and he had no conception of how strongly the repetition of those words was working in Philipson's mind.

"But, if it's not true——" Philipson's voice was less steady than it had been all the time. "How can I find out—for certain?" he cried.

"Look here, Philipson," Mr. Tellwright began. He had found something more to say than a declaration of unbelief. "You say that you have no memory of the time between two and five approximately. Make it one-thirty to five-thirty, for safety, and then that's the only time we've got to bother about. You've got to try and find out who saw you during that time. Peppard's one. We can find out from him when that was exactly. But much the most important thing is to know if you were at Oldners Farm. Did Mrs. Marshall see you there? If she saw you and then saw Marshall after you had gone, you've nothing to worry about."

"I might,'" said Philipson heavily, "have killed him afterwards, somewhere else."

"It doesn't seem to me likely." Mr. Tellwright was obstinate, but again he felt himself inadequate, even to the point of wishing that he had studied some of Justina's library of detective fiction. Another idea struck him. "If you went up to the farm again, mightn't you remember it—I mean *if* anything had happened there?"

"Oh!" said Philipson. He sounded frightened. "You don't understand," he muttered hurriedly, "I—I—I'm afraid even to think of the farm. I can't bear to go near it. That's one of the things that makes me think I must have done—something dreadful there. Yorke thought so too, when I told him. I had to tell him the whole thing."

Mr. Tellwright was not, for the moment, interested in Mr. Yorke.

"Of course, I don't know," he said, "but I should think if you feel that way, it is some subconscious part of your mind which is keeping you away, lest you should remember."

In spite of the dark, Mr. Tellwright knew that Philipson had flinched.

"That's what I think," he said, in a muffled voice.

"But," Mr. Tellwright hastened on, "that doesn't mean that you did the murder. If it is murder. Perhaps you saw it done."

There was silence. Then suddenly Philipson said: "I'll go —I'll go now," and he started off.

"Wait!" said Mr. Tellwright, and Philipson stopped and stood still, stamping his feet between cold and impatience.

The Vicar had remembered that he had a duty to do besides that of helping Philipson to find out whether he were guilty or no. For according to the Vicar's way of thinking, even if he were guilty, Philipson must be resolved not to kill himself.

"Wait," he said again. He had courage and now he needed it. "If you find out—if you find out that the worst is true, what then?"

Philipson did not answer.

"Listen," said the Vicar. "You don't believe as I do. I know that. So if I told you that it is a sin against God for a man to kill himself, it wouldn't mean anything to you. But there's something else. There are people who care for you. If you kill yourself, you'll be—murdering—something in them."

"Are there?" Philipson sounded a little surprised, but not at all bitter.

"Well," said Mr. Tellwright, "I do."

There was a moment's silence. Mr. Tellwright was horrified, not at the words, but at the tone he had used. His mind had been so full of Justina, that his voice had, to his own ear at least, added "and someone else."

Philipson was horrified too—horrified at himself, for having put such an unwarrantable, such a crazy construction upon the Vicar's words. It couldn't be true. Tellwright couldn't have meant, and if he could have meant, would never have hinted at that. Yet, even though it weren't true, the suggestion had power.

He said: "Here—take this. Then you'll know," and shoved a pistol into the Vicar's hand.

Mr. Tellwright would not take it. "No," he pushed it away. "I do know."

"Whatever happens——" Philipson began, and stopped with a jerk; but Mr. Tellwright knew that he had received a promise that would not be broken.

Philipson was turning away, but he pulled up again because he heard, from out of the fog, the murmur of the Vicar's voice, dropped to a tone unfamiliar to him, but well known to the congregation of Benmarsh Church. The words too were strange to Philipson, and he only caught a few of them, but those were beautiful: "Lighten our darkness . . . great mercy . . ."

18

MARTHA DESTROYS AN ALIBI

THAT SUNDAY AFTERNOON Mrs. Tucker was entertaining her cousin Martha, the Vicar's cook, to a royal tea of homemade bread, scones, currant loaf, raisin cake, three sorts of jam, and boiled eggs. Mrs. Tucker was a Yorkshire woman, and when she had guests they did not go away fasting.

Since Martha was in the family the cloistral quiet and chill of Mrs. Tucker's front room was not today disturbed. Mrs. Tucker was very proud of her front room. It was furnished, it was almost completely filled, by a cut-plush suite from the Co-operative Stores, and only by dint of much careful scheming had it been possible to squeeze in a glass cabinet containing china—nondescript, heraldic, or chattily proverbial—a small stool, an insecure folding table, and a complicated bamboo erection designed to support plants, but which Mrs. Tucker preferred to use as something in the nature of a Tree of Jesse. Four generations of Tucker's family and three of Mrs. Tucker's were represented upon various levels of this invention, besides a number of collaterals. The central and most commodious position was however occupied not by any great progenitor, but by a glass case containing two stuffed kingfishers, a canary, and a linnet, all slightly moth-eaten.

Yet, though a source of pride, Mrs. Tucker's front room—
she admitted it herself—was not comfortable, not cosy-like.
So, this cold and dreary Sunday afternoon, she and Martha sat
in the kitchen, newspapers spread on the steel fender, feet
on the newspapers, skirts well turned back to save them from
scorch. Here, at tea time, there was a large and solid table on
which not only food in plenty, but elbows might be planted.
Here, instead of a smell of damp, and paint, and chill, was a
mingled smell of Tucker's tobacco, of Mrs. Tucker's rheu-
matic embrocation, of past and present meals, together with
the complex, indescribable, indivisible smell of pure fug.
Here the fire did not smoke, and the red glow of the open
range was reinforced by radiation from the oven, so that it
became almost a luxury to remember the cold and wet outside.

Martha held out her cup to be re-filled.

"Thank you. I will have another."

Mrs. Tucker swilled the tea leaves briskly round, and
emptied them into the slop basin, which, with the teapot, had
descended to her from her grandmother. The teapot held
enough to satisfy six thirsty men, and the slop basin was the
size of a small bucket. Mrs. Tucker found their capacity con-
venient, though she thought them rather inelegant.

"D'you remember," said Martha, her eyes on the spouting
flow of tea that was almost as densely brown as that drink the
makers proclaim to be beneficial to every individual who can
read. "D'you remember how Effie Thomas used to tell our
fortunes?"

Mrs. Tucker chuckled. "And there was always 'a few tears'?
Yes, I do."

"She said," Martha went on in her harsh, salt voice, "that I
was going to marry a chap with a glass eye. Well I was spared
that anyhow. When I was young and silly I used to think how
awful it would be if he took it out at night. I always thought
he'd pop it into a glass of water, like dad did his teeth. I always
wanted to find out, to be ready like, but I was too shy to ask
any one."

Mrs. Tucker was large, with several chins, but her eyes had

never grown any older than they were when Tucker first met her. She chuckled again like a contented hen, and countered Martha's recollection with another.

"Effie was that proud when I began to walk out with Tucker, because she said she'd read it in me teacup. But I don't know as you could ever have called Tucker 'a tall slight man.'"

Reminiscences of the past were interrupted by the sound of the back door opening. It was the present-day Tucker, tall but certainly not slight, who came in from an industrious and oily hour with his bicycle.

"Late as usual," Mrs. Tucker called out cheerfully.

"Shan't be long, Mother," he replied. "Is Martha there?"

"Aye—I am that, Tom Tucker."

"Tom!" came Tucker's voice. "Get along with y'r 'Tom'— Y're never tired of that joke, Martha."

Martha laughed, and Mrs. Tucker's eyes smiled.

"Get on!" she cried. "Get on, and get yourself clean and come and have y'r tea. Have some plum cake, Martha."

Tucker said: "All right," and retired from the conversation.

"Talking of getting married and such things," said Martha, looking across at her cousin with her crooked, hesitating smile. "I think I know someone who'll be doing it soon. Mind you, I wouldn't say this to any one but you, but I know you and Bob don't talk."

"We don't. There would be things known in Benmarsh if *he* talked," said Mrs. Tucker with complacency, jerking her head towards the scullery, from whence came the trundling of the roller towel. "Who is it?"

"Miss Justina and Mr. Philipson."

"You don't say! What makes you think that?"

"Well," said Martha, "I've been putting two and two together. I had me suspicions before, and then the other day— when I was waiting for the bus to go into Farley, I saw 'em at the end of Marshall's lane. She'd got off her bicycle to talk to him."

The Sergeant did not know that he was listening till he found himself with the comb in his hand, staring into the little mirror that hung on the scullery window frame, and doing nothing about tidying his hair. He pulled himself together and laid on with the comb. There was nothing in Mr. Philipson meeting Miss Justina near Marshall's lane. Why shouldn't he? But—— "Oh damn Peppard!" said Tucker's inmost apprehensive soul.

"They looked so happy and merry together it did yer heart good to see them. And then he went off up the lane to Marshall's, but before he'd got very far he looked back, and she was looking back too. She waved her hand; women is always quicker on the uptake over a thing like that, *I* think, and less like to show shame, though they're shyer in oncoming. But he looked fair caught. I could have laughed."

Martha had taken a big mouthful of cake, and her story was interrupted. But now Tucker was quite certainly and consciously listening. "Marshall's lane—the other day." But which day? Could he get it out of Martha without asking her point blank. He must find out, because if the other day were last Tuesday——? And what time? Tucker, conscious that he was eavesdropping, and feeling guilty, rattled the roller towel again, pulled out a drawer in the dresser, and rummaged in it, but not so loud as to drown Martha's voice.

"You shouldn't have watched, Martha." Mrs. Tucker's rebuke was tempered by what can only be described as a smile in her voice.

Martha swallowed her cake.

"Bless you. They knew I was there. And I couldn't help it. I was waiting for me bus to go in to Farley. That bus is always late on market day. It didn't come by till close on half-past two."

Tucker shut the drawer. So it was last Tuesday. This was real bad. The man that Mrs. Marshall saw must have been Philipson. But then why hadn't she recognized him? And why on earth should he have killed Marshall?

"Are you coming, Dad?" called Mrs. Tucker.

"Yes—in a minute."

But he stood still, puzzled and frowning heavily.

"Well," Mrs. Tucker turned her attention back to Martha's

news, "I hope they'll make it up soon if she likes him. Though I'd have liked to see Miss Justina go off with a man bigger than herself. I've a preference for big men, you see."

Even in his pre-occupation Tucker's eyes twinkled. "The puss!" said something in his brain.

"Oh, he's a nice gentleman is Mr. Philipson," Martha declared, "though that untidy! But he's an artist and I suppose they are like that. Queer things artists—'Stead of drawing Miss Justina he must draw that Mrs. Marshall—I don't like her looks, but the way he talked of her to Miss Justina! I heard him. If I'd been her I'd ha' been that angry. I said to her afterwards I didn't see why Mr. Philipson should want to paint a sly-faced creature like that. She laughed, but I didn't think as she was best pleased herself. But she said it was the slyness he wanted to paint and had I seen her portrait? I hadn't and I didn't want to. Well, Tom Tucker."

But Sergeant Robert Tucker, as he plumped heavily into his chair and fixed his eyes upon a representation of the battle of Inkerman, replied to Martha's pleasantry with not more than a gruff: "Well, Martha!"

Tucker indeed had cause to be glum. He knew that it was owing to his own stupid pig-headedness, that he had been made a fool of. He didn't blame Mr. Yorke, nor yet Mr. Tellwright. It was quite obvious that they had only told him what Mr. Philipson had told them. It was against Mr. Philipson and Mrs. Marshall that Tucker's anger burned, as well as against himself. So angry was he, that as he sat abstractedly munching, he was devising subtleties of approach such as no one would have believed him capable of.

His obvious absent-mindedness acted as a damper on Mrs. Tucker and Martha. His wife indeed guessed that something had turned up to worry him, though what and when, she could not imagine. Martha however felt that his silence indicated a desire to be rid of the visitor, and long before she would ordinarily have thought of taking her leave, in fact while the bells were still ringing for evensong, she got up and said she must go.

"Oh! no," said Mrs. Tucker.

"No, don't," said Tucker. "I'm just going to finish mending that tire. And then I've got to go out, Ma."

"Oh dear!" Mrs. Tucker lamented. She suspected that what took him out was business of the service, therefore unpleasant business, and her suspicions were confirmed when she heard him go into the outer lobby and shut the door; she knew that meant he was ringing up the Police Station at Mallingford. In the intervals of a very cosy chat with Martha she speculated without much curiosity upon the nature of the business, but her speculations, which plunged no deeper than a case of petty larceny or, at the most, assault, fell very far short of the mark.

Yorke was just coming downstairs at Miller's Green when he heard Tucker's ran-tan on the door. He stood still where he was and waited. Mrs. Harker opened the door, learnt that Tucker wanted Mr. Philipson, and informed him sourly that Mr. Philipson had gone out about a quarter of an hour ago. Yorke, listening, heard Tucker's brooding—"Hum!" and his —"Oh well, never mind. I suppose you don't know now where he was going?"

Yorke was gripping the bannister rail. From plain, disabling fear at the first sound of Tucker's voice his mind had leapt to a hope that what Tucker had come to announce was the discovery of the corpse of Philipson. But from that hope he tumbled back into fear. If Tucker were to go looking for Philipson he might find him—too soon. "God!" said Yorke through his teeth. Mrs. Harker was shutting the door. He stepped forward——

"Is that the Sergeant? Wait a minute."

Mrs. Harker had shut the door but she opened it again. "Sergeant Tucker!"

Yorke heard the Sergeant's footsteps return towards the threshold. For a moment he wished he hadn't called him back; he didn't know how he should deal with him, and what new lies he should tell. But something had to be done. He only hoped his face wouldn't twitch, as it had done while he was looking at himself in the glass just now.

"Come in here," he said to the Sergeant, and led the way

into the sitting room. Sergeant Tucker said to himself: "Something's up here, all right."

Yorke shut the door and went over to the fireplace. He seemed to find difficulty in beginning. Then he said:

"You want Mr. Philipson. May I ask why?"

Tucker hesitated. But he decided that Mr. Yorke wouldn't gossip. And anyway, everyone would be gossiping soon.

"Well, sir, it's like this. We have reason to believe that Mr. Philipson *was* at Oldners Farm last Tuesday afternoon. So I must ask him some questions."

Yorke said: "I was afraid of that. I didn't mislead you willingly the other day, Sergeant," he added quickly.

"No, no. Of course not," Tucker reassured him. Evidently Mr. Yorke had been finding out some things lately, and they had upset him. "Would you mind, sir, telling me just what you are afraid of, and why."

Yorke sat down in his chair and put his head in his hands. Whatever Tucker thought, he couldn't help it. He was so tired. A spoiled child, he remembered those days when he had been able, if worsted in a game, to run to his mother, declaring shrilly: "I'm not playing! I'm not playing any more!" He felt that he ought to be able to do it now, if only he knew whom to run to.

But anyway it wasn't Tucker. He'd got to keep Tucker here till Philipson had had time to shoot himself. He began, heavily, to explain that Philipson had been queer—very queer —since last Tuesday. He told Tucker quite a lot more, remembering to put in every now and again such phrases as: "But I hate telling you these things. It's as if I'd been spying on the fellow," or: "It's a beastly business, Sergeant."

At the end of ten minutes Tucker nodded solemnly. "Yes, yes, sir," he soothed the young man, thinking as he did so, how strangely thin-skinned some gentlemen were. "Yes, yes, of course it's right for you to tell me all this."

He paused at the door as Yorke was seeing him out.

"You don't know, sir," he asked in a confidential whisper, "where I'm likely to find Mr. Philipson?"

Yorke put up his fingers to his mouth, so as to hide it, and bit his nails.

"I don't know." (Which way would Philipson certainly *not* have gone?) "Let me see!" (He wouldn't shoot himself in the village street anyway). "Wait a minute! He had a letter in his hand, and he borrowed a stamp from me. He must have been going to post it."

When Tucker had taken himself off in the direction of the village, Yorke went back into the sitting room. Again he dropped into his chair, and again he buried his face in his hands. He was mortally tired; he would have given anything to be able to sit there, drinking a stiff whiskey, with nothing more difficult to face than climbing upstairs to bed.

But instead he had to think; to think hard. God! It was all so complicated, like a child's nest of boxes, one thing inside the other. What to do with old Marshall now? Tucker would want a body.

For a moment he thought: "I'm sunk!" He sat still because he was entirely unable to move. Then it was as if the weight of a mountain had been lifted from him.

Tucker would want a body. Let him have it then! He was welcome to it now Philipson, the suicide, would inevitably be taken for the murderer. So that thing in the fields could stay where it was. It didn't concern Marc Yorke any more.

The relief was so great that he felt for a few moments quite lightheaded. But he did not enjoy it long. A new thought came that fairly hoisted him out of his chair. He had just remembered someone, who, during the last few days, had seemed sufficiently unimportant for him to forget. Mrs. Marshall. He hadn't been near her: it hadn't been safe to go near her since—since Tuesday. But now if Tucker went up to the farm with this idea of Philipson in his head, and he was bound to go, sooner or later, to collect evidence, there was no telling what the woman would say.

"Damn her!" said Yorke viciously. It was indeed, to his way of thinking, all her fault.

He was amazed that he could ever have overlooked this danger. Tucker must have been to the farm already; at the thought of the frightful possibilities of that visit, sweat broke out on his back. But so far she had let nothing out, and now, thank goodness, he had remembered in time.

Mrs. Harker, carrying the supper tray out of the kitchen, was surprised to see Mr. Yorke come hurriedly out of the sitting room and grab his coat and cap from the peg.

He also seemed surprised to see her.

"Forgotten something. Be back soon," he muttered.

She thought his manner strange.

19

SOMETHING COMES TO
LIGHT IN THE DARK

PHILIPSON WAS NOT given to introspection, but when he came abreast of the gate at Miller's Green, he did find it strange to remember that he had not thought to see it again. The notion was sufficiently arresting to make him swing his torch towards it. The light caught the little brass knob of the gate, tarnished and pale with fog; but it missed Sergeant Tucker's bicycle leaning against the railings just beyond.

Not quite twenty minutes later, after a dismal trudge through the half-melted snow, with only a waning hope for company, he reached Oldners Farm, opened the gate, and squeezed through, feeling as he did so the spines of the gooseberry bushes just inside claw at his coat like small, spiteful fingers.

The house in front of him was lightless. His heart sank. If Mrs. Marshall was out, he would have to go back to Miller's Green and wait, and spend another night without knowing—another night. He knocked. He knocked again and again until the reverberation of sound seemed to batter on the inside of his skull, but there was no answer.

At last he turned away. "She *can't* be there," he thought, "I've made enough noise to wake the dead." Well—what now?

He knew what now. He stood still; his mind was like a frightened horse, and he had to get it under control. The Vicar had said that perhaps just being at the farm would make him remember. So if he went down to the stable yard——Something in him cried vehemently: "No! No! Don't go!" But Mr. Tellwright had said that his subconscious mind would try to prevent his remembering. He mustn't let it.

With something approaching physical nausea he moved away towards the stables, picking his way across the yard between heaps of melting sludge which lay where they had been swept together on the first morning of the snow. He swung his torch this way and that. It grabbed up and flung aside a handful, as it were, of the stable door, the corner of a trough, a pile of swedes. But these things meant nothing to him.

"It's no good," he told himself. "I'll have to go back." The small light which the Vicar had kindled in his mind had flickered and gone out, leaving a greater darkness. His hand went into his pocket and touched the pistol, no colder now than his own fingers. But he couldn't use it, since he'd given his word to Tellwright.

The thought of the long and lightless tramp home weighed him down like lead. Should he try the short cut down Green Lane? It would be very bad with the thaw, but anything seemed preferable to the twenty minutes' grind back along the road. He left the yard, with a shiver that was as much mental as physical, and found the stile that led into the Green Lane.

The first part of the lane was not so bad. The snow here was untrodden, so that it was white, and even faintly crisp under his feet. He had gone a couple of hundred yards before he reached the place where, had he only thought of it before, there was always a quagmire except in summer. Now, it was a dark stretch of mud and water perhaps a foot deep in parts. He was in it and had nearly lost a shoe before he realized what he had come on. He floundered, and had to jump back.

Damn! this was the limit! He flashed his torch close to the ground looking for good foothold, but as far as he could see the slough stretched from hedge to hedge. He knew that he would do well to turn back and go round by the road, but with a very common obstinacy, having started, he would hold on. The torch showed him a gap in the briar hedge to his right. He scrambled through it, and went a few paces along the edge of the field beside the lane. This was a different matter. The ground was good, and he was on clean snow again. He pushed on; he did not even need to use his torch, for the field was under plough, and the furrows parallel with the hedge and the lane; he simply walked up one of them.

But at the end of that field his luck finished. There was neither gate nor gap into the next field, nor could he get back into the lane. Again he must choose whether he had better not turn about, and again he went on, deciding to make a cast along the hedge to find a gap or a gate, and then strike diagonally across the next field back to the lane.

He seemed to walk miles along that infernal hedge, stumbling over the ends of the furrows, before he could break through. And then he found himself on soft soggy ground, stubble and grass underfoot, for this field was seed.

The going was bad. The field was trackless. The fog was thick. The journey home, with no hope to help him, was becoming a nightmare. He stopped once, stared round, and listened. He might have been the only man left alive, and all the world reduced to lightless chaos. He thought, but it was no thought, only a gush of fear: "I'll never get back." Panic seized him. All round was fog, empty and blind. If only there had been a hedge alongside it would have been better; a hedge was something solid in the nothingness in which he was drowning. He put his head down and began to run, but the run was not much more than a heavy lurching trot.

He had not gone far when that instinct which is in savages, and in a few civilized persons, pulled him up short. There was something in front of him. He could not have reached the hedge yet, for the field, he knew, was a big one. Yet he was sure that there was something, quite close to him, but hidden in the thick dark. And though he had the torch in his hand he could not bring himself to move his finger upon the switch.

Instead he stood there asking himself what it could be. A fowl house? But Marshall's hens resided in a corner of the stable. A hayrick? Not in the middle of the field. Of course; he had it; it was a scarecrow. At that reasonable suggestion part of his mind withdrew its objection to having a look at it to make sure. His finger slid down the switch.

The yellow glare of the big torch lit up a fading circle of white, thick eddies of fog, and a few paces from him, a scarecrow, tattered black coat, greenish trousers, and battered hat absurdly trimmed with a topknot of melting snow. It was only a scarecrow.

No. It was not only a scarecrow. Philipson felt the back of his head freeze, and his hair go pricking. His eyes moved from the stained dark sacking that made a blotched, featureless mask beneath the hat, to the ends of the crossbar which held stiffly out the arms of the coat; and from there to the lower edge of the draggled trousers. This scarecrow had hands; it wore boots. The sacking under the hat was dark with dried blood; Philipson knew that it hid a face.

He dropped the torch, which burned still as it lay, and flooded the pockmarked snow with a little pool of radiance. Its light just touched the boots, sodden, creased, and crossed one above the other as if in some absurd dance. But Philipson did not see. His hands were crushed over his eyes, while his mind was tossed and tumbled as uncontrollably as a small boat caught in the wake of a liner. Instinctively he knew that in the next few minutes he would either regain command of the memory of those forgotten hours, or lose hold on that, and far more beside.

For a little while it was touch and go. Then the dizzy agitation began to subside. He was shaking; he heard himself, as if it had been another man, drawing long gasping breaths, but he was in possession once more of all his past except for one black blot of plain unconsciousness.

He did not uncover his eyes till the recaptured memory had arranged itself, startlingly minute and orderly in his mind.

It was Tuesday afternoon. He had gone up Green Lane. He was in the Marshalls' farmyard. It was empty and the stable and barn doors closed. He had thought—(even that came back to him as if it had happened an hour ago)—"I bet they're all gone to Farley market," and then: "Damn Yorke's honey!"

He was just crossing the yard towards the house, intending to knock and make sure that no one was at home, when his painter's eye was caught by the fine, cool gold of some new straw that trailed out from under the stable door. It looked so bright upon the sodden dark cobbles of the yard that he stepped aside to enjoy the colour.

It was only then that he saw another colour spattered on the gold—a royal sanguine. Whatever was it? And what was the battering and stamping that was going on inside the stable.

He had not been uneasy so much as idly curious, but now he saw something that startled him. A little pool of darker red, so dark as to be almost black, stood in a joint of the uneven, dirty paving. As he looked, the edges of the pool moved. It was widening and creeping towards him.

His thought was: "Someone's been savaged by a horse." He tore open the upper half of the door. The stable was dim, and full of the strong soft smell of hay, horseflesh and manure. An old, flea-bitten grey, its ears back and nostrils quivering, was sidling about in its stall. Now and again it lashed out so that the timbers rang.

But no one lay, as he had feared to see, within reach of its hoofs. He pushed into the stable and looked round. To his left, leaning against the wall, was a half-made scarecrow, the coat stretched wide on the crossbar, a battered hat lying on the ground beside it and a ball of twine. To the right of the door was a pile of straw, from which the trailing wisps extended as far as the threshold and beyond. It was from under the straw that the blood came in a slow, narrow stream.

For a second he dared not. Then he was lifting the straw to see.

He saw. A smashed face, horrible, and made more horrible by the chaff and bits it was stuck with, lay underneath.

He backed away, his hands to his eyes, but still he saw it, and not only this wreck and ruin of a man, but that other, seen years ago, in the dust of a shell hole.

So interlocked were these two sights that he hardly knew where he was, almost indeed, was awaiting the blast of the shell which seven years ago had wiped out, for a time, memory and reason.

The stable was rocking round him. He couldn't keep his feet. He stumbled, hit his shoulder on the post of the stall, and found himself on one knee. Something told him: "Look out! That horse's hoofs!" He ducked instinctively; there was a crash that split the world in two, and then blackness.

What he remembered next was hazy, because it was blackened over by physical pain. He was crawling on all fours to the door, saying to himself: "I mustn't be sick." Something was hammering inside his head which might break it open any minute.

Then he was on his feet outside the door, carefully, clumsily, laboriously trying to shut the two halves; but the top one would not shut, so he gave up trying, because every time he slammed it the noise was a fresh blow.

That was what had happened last Tuesday, that, and an unsteady, trailing retreat up Footpad Hill, towards Ipsden Woods, all with that blinding headache that would not let him think nor see, an innocent man, though his hands were bloody.

He took his fingers from his eyes, and saw at his feet the little still pool of brightness welling from the torch. It startled him by the mere loveliness of light, that primary loveliness which irresistibly draws all human eyes.

Mr. Tellwright had said: "Lighten our darkness." At that moment, it was obvious to Philipson, though more doubtful afterwards, that the Vicar's request had been listened to, and that it had been answered.

The slushy, sodden field had seemed to clutch and cling to his feet as he had come. When he went back it might have been dry turf. He crept through a gap that on any other occasion he would have judged suitable for nothing larger than a rabbit; he lost his hat but that didn't matter. Nothing could stop him. He was on his way back to Miller's Green, and to life.

20

TUCKER SAYS "HOMICIDAL MANIA!"

WHEN SERGEANT TUCKER left Miller's Green, he did not, though he turned his bicycle in the direction of the village, intend to make his way to the post office, in the hope of finding Mr. Philipson there, or of meeting him on the return journey. Mr. Yorke had clearly seen nothing strange in such haphazard tactics, but although that gentleman had shown himself quite intelligent and helpful in the earlier stages of the business, it was evident to Tucker that he had now fairly got the jumps; and the suggestion of hunting Mr. Philipson through the dark of a foggy night was just silly.

What Tucker intended, and what he did, was to go home, telephone to Mallingford, report the unexpected developments of the case, and ask that Mallingford railway station should be watched.

"Right! Right! O.K." He heard the voice of the Superintendent at the other end. "Very well, Sergeant. Can't do much else till you get hold of the man."

"No, sir, but I thought I'd go up to the farm and question the woman again you know."

The telephone said: "Right," into his ear again, clucked and was silent. The "Super" never did waste words.

As Tucker drove his bicycle slowly through the fog, he reflected gloomly upon what he called to himself "a very nasty business." It was not only that if his suspicions were justified he would soon have to arrest for murder a gentleman with whom he had been on polite, if not cordial terms; and a woman too—a thing which Tucker always disliked. Besides the unpleasantness, there were obscurities in the case that puzzled him. If Philipson and Mrs. Marshall were in it to-gether, why had she ever let on that there had been a man there that afternoon, and even insisted that he had gone off in the very direction that Philipson had taken? And if that man had been Philipson, why on earth had he not washed off the traces of the crime? Murderers, so far as Tucker knew, don't generally ramble about the country literally red-handed.

The thought of the blood on Philipson's hands reminded Tucker of Peppard. How Peppard will crow, he thought bit-terly, and his gorge rose. The only comfort was, that though the murder would be, as it were, Peppard's property, he had not guessed the collusive guilt of Mrs. Marshall. That thought maintained the Sergeant through a very dreary ride; that, and the hope that if Mrs. Marshall were in the same state of nerves as he had found her on his last visit, there was a good chance that he might startle her into a full confession.

It was therefore a sad disappointment to him when he found, as Philipson had found not quite ten minutes earlier, that there was no sign of life or light at all at Oldners Farm. But Tucker, no more than Philipson, was content to leave without making sure that Mrs. Marshall was out. He went up to the door and rapped heavily.

He got no answer. "She's out," he thought, and then—he glowered at the door—"Have the two of them cleared out to-gether?"

He felt over the surface of the wood till his fingers found the latch. It clicked, and the door swung partly open.

Tucker said something under his breath. This looked in-deed as though they had. He pulled out his torch and switched it on. The little passage, filled with the white glare of light, was silent and empty.

"Mrs. Marshall!" he shouted.

"Any one in?" he shouted again, and answered himself: "No one."

After a moment's thought he stepped over the threshold and shut the door behind him. If the woman had bolted, the sooner they knew the better; and the open door gave him enough justification for making an entry.

The kitchen door was to his left. He looked in. The sliding light of his torch fell upon the fireplace, quenching a lurking gleam of red with its whiter radiance. But he could see that the fire was not quite out, so she must have been here today. The scullery door was opposite to him. He crossed the kitchen and pushed it open. The room was dank and very cold; there was a sudden scurry and rustle in one corner; a rat, disturbed by the noise and light, whisked off behind the pump. Tucker disliked rats. "Grr!" he shouted, and shut the door.

Not much use really, he told himself, looking round down here. It was upstairs, in the bedrooms, where he would find signs of any hurried flight. He left the kitchen, and moving quietly in the forbidding silence of the house, climbed the stairs.

The first door he opened was certainly that of the Marshalls' bedroom. The bed was tossed over, half made; a pair of shoes, caked with farmyard mud, lay dropped on the linoleum. Round about the room, reflecting the torchlight with a dull, blurred gleam, stood some big pieces of old mahogany furniture: a washstand with a marble top heavy enough for a tombstone: a chest of drawers: a wardrobe adorned with ponderous volutes. Tucker pulled open one of the wardrobe doors and peered into the musty recesses. There were coats and trousers belonging to old Marshall, and draggled frocks of his wife, but no sign of a hasty flitting. When he shut the door, it gave a long squeal as of pain and protest, which, even to Tucker's steady nerves, sounded unduly loud in the quiet.

He went downstairs again. He had drawn blank, and wasted his time. He stood for a second with his finger on the latch of the front door; he pressed it down, then let it rise again. Had he heard, or had he only thought he heard, a slight sound in the stillness of the house? The light of his torch raked the passage again. If he *had* heard something the sound came from behind the door opposite that of the farm kitchen. He went back and opened it.

The first thing he saw was a mounting cheerful flame in the grate opposite to him; a banked fire had just fallen in, and it must have been the sound of its collapse which had reached him. The second thing he saw was the hearthrug dragged all askew as though someone had tripped over it. The third thing was a broken flowerpot which lay between the hearthrug and a gimcrack table in the middle of the room. Soil was spilled out of the pot over the folds of a green plush table cloth that lay tumbled on the floor, and an aspidistra poked one unbroken leaf out of the confusion in a forlorn jollity.

Tucker stepped quickly into the room, and swept the light of the torch over the floor beyond the table.

"Phew!" he said. "Smashed to blazes!"

He was not looking at the plant or pot, but at the head of the woman who lay on the threadbare carpet.

Tucker, his face wooden, but his stomach queasy, knelt down by her. Mrs. Marshall had not cleared out.

He was by no means a fanciful man, but when he stood for a moment outside the locked door of Oldners Farm, he drew several unusually deep breaths, because the air, though thick with fog, was cold, clean, and pure. Then he made for his bicycle, the dim gleam of whose lamp he could just make out where he had left it in the road. His job now was to find the murderer; and he was the man, unless Tucker were a Dutchman, who had killed old Marshall too.

The gate of Oldners Farm had at some time lost one of its hinges, and the deficiency had been supplied with a bit of rope. It was, consequently, tricky to open, and when Tucker tried it, it would not budge. He swore under his breath, and fished out his torch again to see what was holding the gate. But the light fell on something which interested him far more.

A large handkerchief trailed limply from the spines of the gooseberry bushes which had caught it; a large, dark blue silk handkerchief with a printed Paisley pattern. Tucker took it carefully from the clinging thorns and looked it over. There was a name in one corner. The little scarlet letters of Cash's frilling were quite clear in the light of the torch——

"P. Philipson."

Tucker rode his bicycle back to Benmarsh at a pace which, considering the fog, was disgracefully dangerous, and might well have landed him in a ditch had he not known the ground so well, and had not the right-angled bends of the road been marked for him by the lighted windows of Mr. Tellwright's parishioners seated at their Sunday suppers. At the first turn two windows in the Manor Farm glowed warmly at him; at the next a small blink proceeded from a cottage; at the next a wide haze of light welled from the open doorway of Mr. Heap's bungalow. The next stretch of road was straight until he got to the A.A. Box on the main road, and Miller's Green stood to the right of it, halfway along. He put on an extra spurt of speed.

Then he jammed on the brakes. Approaching him was a car; he could hear both the sound of the engine and frequent blasts on the horn; either a nervous driver, Tucker thought, or one who did not know the road well. He found the grass verge and clung to it, riding slowly and peering ahead. But no lights came down on him. Instead the sound of the car ahead changed and grew louder, then suddenly diminished again. It must have turned into Miller's Green drive. Sure enough, when Tucker drew abreast of the drive a second or two later, he could hear a standing car panting and palpitating in the yard behind; he could see the glow from its lights too.

It was not, however, the knowledge that Mr. Yorke had presumably just driven in, that brought Tucker off his bicycle, and set him fumbling for the little brass knob of the gate. He had noticed that the sitting-room window showed a light through a long gash between the curtains. Ten to one the light denoted the presence of Mr. Philipson, since the engine of the car had only this moment been switched off, and Mr. Yorke had not had time to reach the house.

Tucker laid hold of the iron door knocker, but he did not raise it. Instead of the heavy ran-tan he intended, another, a far louder noise, split the dark and sent up the rooks from the bare trees across the road in a frenzy of flapping and calling. It was the sound of a pistol shot. For one half second Tucker stood gaping. Then, lugging out his torch, he took to his heels along the front of the house.

As he doubled the corner into the yard it seemed to be full of people, scores of them, but when he stood and flashed the torch systematically over the crowd it resolved itself into five persons. Two maids peered out of the lit doorway at the back of the house. Mr. Tellwright was a little in front of them, also staring into the darkness. Mr. Yorke stood with his back to the silent and lightless car, his arms thrown wide and palms pressed against it. Mr. Philipson, flat and limp, lay with his head on the edge of the old stone drain that crossed the yard.

Yorke said, in a high, sudden voice that was almost a shout:

"He came at me. I'd just got out of the car. I switched off the lights and he came at me in the dark. He'd a pistol in his hand. I caught his wrist, and it went off."

He stopped with a jerk and turned his head to look at Philipson and at Tucker who was kneeling by him. Then he began again in the same voice, though it was a little higher in tone and a little louder.

"He came at me. I saw he'd got a pistol and I switched out the lights. I caught his wrist——"

Tucker rose from his knees, scooping up at the same time the little automatic that lay just wide of Philipson's outspread right hand.

"That's all right, sir," he said sharply, "that's all right. I can see what happened." "And keep your hair on!" he thought.

He found that Mr. Tellwright had crossed the yard and was standing beside him. By the faint light that came from the kitchen door Tucker could see his face. There were no hysterics here, but the look on it frightened the Sergeant.

"It's all right, sir. You'd better sit down a bit," he said hastily.

Mr. Tellwright put the advice by with a shake of his head, though he had to lay his hand on Tucker's outstretched arm.

"Is—Mr. Philipson—dead?"

Tucker said: "No—but he looks middling bad."

"What——" the Vicar forced out the words. "What has happened? I came to see him."

"I tell you." Yorke broke out again shrilly—— "He came——"

Tucker checked him with a fierce: "Will you be quiet!" then turned again to Mr. Tellwright.

"I'm afraid, sir, there's not much doubt that it was Mr. Philipson as killed old Marshall. And now, tonight, he's got Mrs. Marshall too. *And* had a go at Mr. Yorke. It looks to me like as if it's homicidal mania."

He broke off because one of the maids—Agnes—began to laugh. It was a silly giggle at first but it rose till she was laughing, as Tucker told Mrs. Tucker that night, "like a bloomin' hyena."

The Sergeant did not know that the events of the evening had played upon his nerves, but he found Agnes' hysterics simply intolerable.

"Stop that!" he bawled at her, and to Mr. Yorke, "come on. Get her indoors. Take her other arm."

Yorke came on with a jerk. Together they laid hold of Agnes, and bundled her into the house. Mrs. Harker followed.

When they had gone, Mr. Tellwright, who found that he really could not stand any longer, got somehow across the yard to Yorke's car and sat down on the running board. From there he looked back to the place where Philipson lay, beyond the faint light which came from the kitchen door, as if already he belonged to a limbo of lost and forgotten souls. The Vicar dropped his head down upon his hands. All that Philipson had dreaded was true.

He sat there for several minutes before the Sergeant came back to the kitchen door, peered this way and that, and finally flashed his torch across the yard.

"Oh, there you are, sir," he said, with an aggressive but well meant cheerfulness, and he came over to Mr. Tellwright's side.

"Now," he went on, "Mr. Yorke'll take you home in a minute in his car. I'm just waiting for the police ambulance from Mallingford." He hesitated. The situation was, to his mind, delicate. He was uncertain whether it would be correct to appear to notice the Vicar's distress, occasioned as it was by his tenderness for a murderer. "We'll—— He'll——" he began and stopped. "I'll take care of him," he said, roughly and loudly, and in his embarrassment he laughed.

Mr. Tellwright did not, in spite of the laugh, mistake his kindly intention.

"Thank you, Tucker," he said. But there was something which he must find out.

"Did he shoot her?" he asked. He was remembering how he himself had thrust back the pistol into Philipson's hand.

Tucker, startled by the abruptness of the question, answered it crudely.

"Bashed in her head. With the poker. I couldn't find it, but the whopping old one was missing from the kitchen. I doubt if we'll ever find it, but that's what he used, you bet."

The Vicar gave a gasping sigh.

"He wanted to kill himself. I stopped him. I persuaded him to go to the farm," he said: "I'd better tell you."

Simply and very briefly he told Tucker what Philipson had told him.

"That was what he was afraid of, you see," he concluded.

Tucker nodded his head slowly. Mr. Yorke had come out of the house and now stood beside them.

"Poor devil," said Tucker. And then, to Yorke: "It's what I thought. Case of mania. Homicidal."

"Mania. Homicidal," Yorke repeated stupidly. "I never thought of that."

In the silence that followed they all heard the sound of a car approaching, the long sobbing hoot of a horn, and the scrape of brakes.

"Police ambulance," said Tucker unnecessarily, and left them.

He came back with two policemen and a stretcher. Mr. Tellwright saw them stoop over Philipson. They lifted him up, and carried him off, Tucker walking alongside.

Yorke went with them. He was telling Sergeant Tucker that though he had never dreamt that Philipson's was a case of mania, several incidents had occurred which he now saw would be explained only by that hypothesis. "It's terrible. Poor fellow," Mr. Tellwright heard him say.

"It'll be a good thing for him," Tucker rumbled in answer as they turned the corner of the house, "if he kicks the bucket."

Mr. Tellwright let his face drop again into his hands. "Good thing. Good thing." The words babbled themselves through his brain. He had prevented Philipson killing himself. "A good thing." The Vicar's mind sank down into a place where there was no light at all, but only the black imagination of another man's shipwreck.

21

THE VICAR ENTERTAINS A MURDERER

AND JUSTINA! THAT thought ran, poignant, through the leaden misery of his mind. It was so acute a pain that action was a necessity to him. He pulled himself up by the handle of the car door; but the handle dipped under his weight and the door swung partly open. He had moved without any special intention, but now the instinct that had brought him to his feet drove him, like a sick animal, to hide from the pain within him in a privacy of darkness. Slowly, because of his physical weakness, he set one foot on the running board, and stooping crept into the rear of the car.

Something hard and round on the floor rolled under his foot. He stumbled, threw out a hand, caught at nothing, and fell sprawling on the back seat.

For a few moments the shock, and the effort he had made to save himself, deprived him of breath and thought. He sat, only waiting for the commotion of his heart to subside. It quieted. He was able to breathe without pain. With the relief, curiosity wakened. He stooped carefully and felt about the floor for the round hard ball on which he had stumbled. His fingers groped over the tufty rough floor covering. They met something, but it was a bar, not a ball; a long smooth bar of iron. He felt down it. It thickened and roughened at one end.

He felt up it. At this end there was a rough knob, that was not exactly wet, but sticky.

He snatched his fingers away. The notion that had come into his mind seemed for a moment to numb it, then to set it racing. One hand went to the pocket where he kept his pipe lighter and pulled it out, the other drew the door of the car softly to without shutting it. Then, but not before his knuckles touched the floor, his index finger moved on the little wheel of the lighter. The faint pulsating flame with its fount of spirituous blue glimmered over his shoes, over the brown carpeting of the car, and over the thing that lay at his feet. He flipped back the cap and there was darkness again. But in the darkness he saw still the long heavy kitchen poker, its knob dulled with the same dark stuff that smeared his own finger tips. It was in that instant that he heard, from beyond the house, the sound of the police ambulance driving off.

He heard the sound, marked, and afterwards interpreted it; but at the moment he was contemplating with a strained intensity the discovery he had just made; fumbling, like a blind man in an unknown room, to find the key to its import.

He found it by a leap of intuition. Reason came after, crowding argument on argument. The poker Tucker wanted to find was in Yorke's car. Yorke only could have put it there. Yorke had been at Oldners Farm last Tuesday, Tucker had said so. Yorke had made no effort to prevent Philipson committing suicide. And Yorke had lied when he said just now that he had never dreamt Philipson could be suffering from homicidal mania, for Philipson himself had told Yorke what he dreaded. Yorke was a liar. Yorke was the murderer.

The Vicar reached that conclusion in less than half a minute, and he acted on it at once. With a promptness that any man of action might have envied, he laid his hand on the door and pushed it open. He must bring back Tucker. And then he remembered that he had heard the departure of the ambulance.

The police had gone. The murderer remained—and the Vicar.

Mr. Tellwright's heart was groggy, but it was undaunted.

As quickly as he dared move, he got out of the car, shutting
the door behind him with the utmost cautious gentleness.
When, a few minutes later, Yorke came out of the house by
the kitchen door, the Vicar was sitting on the running board
where Yorke had left him. It was not wholly in a pretence of
weakness that he sat stooping forward, his head bent down
over his knees.

Yorke was full of apology and commiseration. He helped
Mr. Tellwright into the car, telling him how sorry, how *frightfully* sorry he was. He left it to the Vicar to decide whether he
was sorry for keeping him waiting, or because Philipson had
been arrested by the police.

Mr. Tellwright, however, did not trouble to resolve the
doubt. Yorke's hands on the steering wheel were without
gloves, and from them came a pleasant smell of scented soap.
The Vicar could guess why he had washed them and it reminded him of the smudges upon his own handkerchief,
where he had hastily wiped his finger tips. The thought pro-
voked something like a shudder in his brain but, fearing lest it
should be transmitted, *via* his arm and coat sleeve, to Yorke's
coat sleeve, arm and brain, he smothered it hastily and
plunged into conversation. If—incredible as it seemed—Yorke
had indeed forgotten for the moment what it was that lay
behind him on the floor of the car, he must not be given a
minute to remember. Whatever happened, yes, *whatever
happened*, he must have no opportunity to dispose of that
piece of evidence which should save Philipson's life and reason.

Years after the Vicar could remember just what he had said,
and just what Yorke had replied, in relation to every yard of
the road between Miller's Green and the Vicarage. It was at
the end of the field with the sandpit in it that Yorke had said
he supposed this—this awful business of poor Philipson was
due to his being shell-shocked during the war. It was just as
the glare of the headlights swung over the osier patch before
the Ferry field, that the Vicar asked when Philipson had
begun to act strangely. Yorke's account of a conversation with
Philipson, in which the latter had spoken about old Marshall

with what Yorke now realized to be crazy violence, had begun at the corner of the Vicarage garden. Then the car turned slowly into the Vicarage gates and pulled up at the door.

Yorke swung out and laid hold of the bell. The Vicar wasn't going to let him get back into his seat. Shaky as to his legs, but with something taut and daring dancing in his brain, Mr. Tellwright got down, and across the porch, and joined Yorke on the doormat just as Martha opened the door.

It was Tellwright, not the younger man, who took charge of the situation.

"Martha, Mr. Yorke has been kind enough to bring me home. I'm afraid I've been very tiresome. But he has been most kind." He turned to Yorke with his gentle yet compelling courtesy. "And you must prove that you forgive me by coming in for a little while."

His hand was on Yorke's arm. Yorke let himself be drawn inside the door. Martha shut it behind them.

"Now," said Mr. Tellwright, when Yorke was sitting in the same roomy chair in which Philipson had sat last Tuesday evening, "Now I'll get you something to drink. It will do us both good. This has been a great shock to me, and I'm sure to you."

He talked himself to the door, and paused there. Would Yorke wonder why—would he suspect why his host went out to fetch the whiskey himself? Mr. Tellwright, who had never before discovered in himself any capacity for impromptu lying, was surprised to hear his own voice go on:

"You must excuse me for a moment. I'll have to fetch it. You see I didn't think one ought to put temptation in the way of the servants." He fumbled in a pocket, produced a key and dangled it for Yorke to see. It was the key of a cupboard in the vestry, but Yorke wouldn't know that; nor would he know that the Vicar's whiskey bottle sat openly upon the sideboard in the dining room from month to month. But, having thus aspersed Martha's character, Mr. Tellwright's probity compelled him to qualify his implication. "Not that Martha isn't the soul of honesty," he said hastily. "But you understand ——"

Yorke thought: "Fussy old bird!" and said: "Of course, yes, quite, don't bother about me."

When the Vicar had gone, shutting the door after him, Yorke let his eyes close, and sank into a state almost of lethargy. He was tired—tired to death. He knew that he could not stay here; that he'd have to get up soon, and begin to think and plan and calculate. But for just a few minutes he would be still, and rest. Things, he told himself, had so far gone better than he could have hoped. Whatever Philipson remembered, he would not be listened to now, a homicidal maniac with two murders to his account. And Mrs. Marshall —she was nothing—nothing at all. He would forget that she had ever existed. He shut his eyes tight, shut his mind and lay supine. He would not think of what had happened in the little parlour, or that nausea, which had almost disabled him on the long, staggering, devious drive back to Miller's Green, might return.

Mr. Tellwright came back. He carried a tray on which stood a siphon, a decanter, and two glasses that jingled together. Putting the tray down he went to the door, and shut it with a slam. He had told Martha not to make any noise going out, but it was better to take no chances. Then he set himself to talk.

At first it was easy enough. "How d'you like it?" and that sort of thing. And Yorke—who must have forgotten—surely would not try to go till he had finished his drink. But the Vicar did not know how long he would have to keep his guest amused and forgetful. As he talked, of the weather, of whiskey, and the budget, Mr. Tellwright's mind was like broken water, catching dozens of different reflected images.

It was:

"Yes, I believe you can still get it at half the price we pay and I don't know how much over proof in the Channel Islands."

How long would it take Martha to get to Tucker's house?

"No—did you?"

And would she be able to get Tucker on the phone at Mallingford at once?

"Yes. I suppose there is a good deal of smuggling."

And would the message be sufficient to convince the Superintendent there of the urgency of the summons?

"No. I've never tasted poteen."

Thank God it's Martha, not any ordinary maid!

"Yes. Some people prefer Irish to Scotch."

Could I have said anything else to bring them, and bring them quickly?

"You don't? Nor I."

Suppose he remembers, how shall I stop him going off? If I have to try force will he—do me in too? That idea, bizarre but not impossible, almost put the Vicar off his stroke, but he recovered himself.

"No—I don't know Scotland well at all. You're going soon for salmon fishing, you say?"

"Yes. Next month. Always do," said Yorke and, by the cool casualness of his tone entirely upset the balance of the Vicar's mind.

This man, lounging here, drinking whiskey, and talking of his holiday, couldn't have committed two—perhaps three murders. Philipson, stammering out his tormenting fears, was infinitely more like what Mr. Tellwright thought a murderer must be.

While the Vicar fought with his doubts, the conversation hung upon a dead centre. There was silence. Like an embarrassed hostess, whose flow of small talk has congealed, he cast about for an occupation. The fire had fallen sulky. He fumbled among the fire irons, and then began to poke it, hastily and noisily.

A movement behind startled him. Yorke had leapt to his feet.

The Vicar turned. He did not drop the poker, but still grasped it as he stood up. Yorke faced him. Mr. Tellwright knew then that what he had begun to think impossible was true; and that Yorke had remembered.

For one long second they looked at each other, and neither could move. But the Vicar was the better man. He sat down again, and though the stroke was rather wild, resumed his battery upon the fire.

"Don't go!" he said, and the tension of his mind was such that he almost laughed at the complete sincerity of his own words.

"I must."

Yorke spoke abruptly. But out of the corner of his eye the Vicar saw that he had picked up his glass again. Still standing he swallowed the remaining whiskey.

"He doesn't *know* that I know," Mr. Tellwright told himself. "He's not sure. He daren't let me suspect anything. But he'll go now."

He was right. Yorke moved quickly towards the door. The Vicar, however, got there first, laid hold on the handle and stood with his back to it. He might, equally well, be keeping the door shut in Yorke's face, or about to open it for him. For a moment, or a few moments at most, since Yorke was not sure, he might delay him yet.

"I'll see you out. I won't bother Martha. We like her to have her evenings to herself as much as possible," he said, and fumbled in his mind for something, indeed for anything to say.

What added to the difficulty was that Mr. Tellwright's ego found itself suddenly divided. He had been fighting against Yorke for Philipson's sake, and loyalty to his friends was bred in the Vicar's bones. But because he was a priest, as well as a gentleman, every man, even every murderer, even Yorke, was sheep of his pasture. The schism went down to the roots of the Vicar's being and for a few seconds swept his mind blank.

In desperation he clutched at the first thought that came. Martha had told Justina a story; Justina had told it to him, *in camera*. Yorke might well think it an odd story for a parson to repeat, but Mr. Tellwright was past caring for that.

"You know, Yorke," he said, "Martha is a remarkable woman—Lancashire born—and they have nimble wits there, I understand. Well, Martha has a niece, and I fear she does not consider the girl's intelligence a credit to the family. When Martha went home for her holidays last year this young person had just bought her first pair of corsets—I understand that they are still called corsets—(You must go? I won't keep you a minute. It's really rather funny.) The girl, it seems, put on the—garment—upside down. Martha, telling my daughter of the incident said: 'And I said to her, what did you think the suspenders were for? To hold your hat on?' "

Yorke had his hand stretched out to turn the handle of the door. He managed to laugh. So did Mr. Tellwright, and his laugh was the better imitation. Then they both stopped laughing abruptly. A door—the Vicar knew that it was the front door—had opened and shut, and there were footsteps in the hall. The Vicar knew them for Martha's, but there was someone with her who trod with a heavy clank upon the tiled floor.

He moved at last, and pulled the study door open, realizing, with surprise and some shame, that his legs were trembling so much that he could hardly stand.

Sergeant Tucker seemed to fill the doorway. In his hand he held a long and heavy kitchen poker.

"Now then, sir," he said, with annoyance in his tone, "will you please tell me where you found this, and who *is* the murderer?"

Mr. Tellwright felt that it was all too crudely melodramatic to be real. Yet it was real. He was playing a game, but the stakes were Philipson's life and sanity.

"I found it," he said, and turned his face to Yorke, "in his car. And he——"

There was no need to say more. At the sight of Tucker, Yorke had backed away till the Vicar's desk stopped him. He stood for a moment, his jaw working, but no words coming. Then suddenly and shockingly, he began to cry.

"I didn't. I didn't. Yes, I did. But I couldn't help it. She——"

Tucker, dragging out his notebook, broke in with a loud and startling gabble:

"You - are - not - compelled - to - say - anything - but - anything - you - say - will - be - taken - down - in - writing - and - may - be - given - in - evidence."

The caution did not check Yorke. He plumped down in

the Vicar's chair, and went on, wringing his hands, and crying, and talking. Most of it was about Mrs. Marshall. The whole business, from start to finish, he gave Tucker to understand, was her fault. The only parts for which she was not responsible were the really clever devices which had baffled the police, and which, with ordinary luck, he insisted, would have continued to baffle them. Upon these Yorke, with a faint but spiteful defiance, was still inclined to plume himself.

"You didn't guess when I showed you that envelope," he taunted the Sergeant. "You didn't guess that I found it on the chimney piece at the farm that afternoon, and posted it myself. And it was a letter from old Marshall telling me he'd had enough of me coming to the farm after his wife. And you didn't guess why I got you to drag Pilly's Pond. Peppard guessed what I meant to do, though he didn't know it was me. He's clever. He's cleverer than you, a lot."

Tucker, like a judicious chairman who checks an indiscreet speaker, stood up, and laid his hand on Yorke's shoulder.

"That's enough. You'd best come along with me."

Yorke got slowly to his feet. But he had not finished.

"And even now you don't know where old Marshall is; though you can see him, any one can see him from Green Lane."

Tucker rose to that. He could not resist it.

"Well, where is he then?" he snapped.

"Keeping the birds off his own field!" said Yorke.

Tucker looked blank. It was Mr. Tellwright who guessed.

"A scarecrow!" he said.

Tucker said: "I'm damned."

But Yorke had begun to laugh, a high cackling laugh. Tucker turned and struck him smartly with the flat of his hand between the shoulder blades.

"That'll do," he said sharply. "And now come along."

22

JUSTINA CANNOT FIND
HER HANDKERCHIEF

PHILIPSON HALF WAKENED in a room he did not know. It was night, but there was a lamp somewhere beyond a screen that cut off most of his view. He was not, however, nearly so much interested in his surroundings as in his physical sensations, which were painful, and complicated by a burning thirst that consumed him. He tried to speak, but the noise he made was not any word. Yet it served, for someone came from behind the screen and gave him something to drink. He went to sleep again immediately.

The next time he woke up it was daylight. He was more ready now to take notice of things, and he began to wonder what had happened to him, and where on earth he was. What had happened he remembered pretty easily and he shut his eyes again and felt very queer for a bit, but when he opened them again it was to go on wondering where he had got to.

The room was high and light, with a satin striped paper, and bunches of flowers between the stripes. It was shabby. The curtains were old printed cotton with a pattern of dull red leaves; when he cautiously turned his head the washstand came into view. The basin and ewer were ornamented with a bunch of rather muddy coloured orange flowers, perhaps meant for poppies. The whole room in fact was artistically lamentable, but to Mr. Philipson most reassuring. For one thing was certain; wherever he was, he was not in any kind of institution whatever, neither in a prison, nor in an asylum, nor even in a hospital.

Yet, when he wakened again, the first thing he saw was a hospital nurse standing beside the edge of the screen. Her back was towards him, and she was mixing something in a medicine glass.

"I say——" Philipson began, and stopped because the faintness of his voice surprised him.

The nurse turned round. It was Justina.

"You're awake," she said, and though her voice was so familiar, Philipson, had he been less bemused, might have recognized a note in it which he did not know, for Justina was now on duty. "Are you feeling better?" Her tone suggested that he must be. And it was true. He said, as loudly and firmly as he could: "Yes——thanks." And then: "Where am I?"

"Dad brought you home," she told him, and then, giving him no time for any more questions:

"Drink this." She stood over him while she firmly and efficiently tipped it down his throat.

"Now go to sleep," she said.

Mr. Philipson blinked at her. He was indeed, very sleepy, and after nearly a week of nights such as the last that he remembered, it was very good to sleep, and a pity indeed to waste any opportunity. Yet, before he dropped back into the feathery deeps he opened his eyes.

"Have you killed that patient of yours so soon?" he asked.

Justina—it was Justina and not the nurse—laughed. And it was Justina's lips that trembled. But Mr. Philipson did not see that, nor did he know, how when he was asleep, his nurse left him, though only to stand on the landing and call softly but urgently:

"Dad! Dad!"

Mr. Tellwright, who had been sitting with the study door open, came up the stairs more quickly than any one would have expected.

"He's all right. His brain—— He's recognized me and re-members things. He's all right," said Justina breathlessly, and whisked back into the patient's room where there was no one to see her face.

It was true that Mr. Tellwright had brought Philipson to the Vicarage, or more precisely, that he had caused him to be brought. When Yorke had been handcuffed and removed, Mr. Tellwright reminded Tucker of the story which Philip-son had told him. He asked Tucker didn't he think that if a man, fearing insanity, and having suffered a severe nervous shock, returned to consciousness in the atmosphere of a hos-pital, the possibility was that—well——? The Vicar left it to Tucker's imagination. Tucker admitted that he would not have thought of that for himself, but that there was something in it. He did not guess that there was also, in the Vicar's mind, something, or rather someone, behind it, namely Justina. The Vicar knew well what would be expected of him from that quarter. In the end Mr. Tellwright had carried his point. Philipson was brought by police ambulance to the Vicarage, and the District Nurse summoned. And even while the bed-room was being got ready for Mr. Philipson, Justina had rung up to say that she would be home next day, as her patient had to go into hospital for an operation.

Only a week after his encounter with Yorke did Philipson become conversational and curious. Justina was sitting at the end of his bed, apparently intent upon some sewing, but she knew, some time before he spoke, that he was getting ready to ask questions.

"Miss Tellwright!"

She bit off a piece of thread: "Yes, Mr. Philipson."

He came straight to the point.

"Are people still thinking that I killed old Marshall?"

"No," said Justina emphatically. "They know you didn't."

"Did you?" he asked in a different tone.

Justina knew what he meant, but the question was a facer. So she pretended not to understand.

"Did I what?"

"Think that I had," said Philipson, not much more explicitly.

Justina felt that she could not go on pretending, but how to answer she did not know. Even had he been a mere acquaintance it would have been awkward to admit that she almost had thought it. But the real difficulty was that he must not guess at the misery she had suffered in thinking it. She took refuge in a superficial candour.

"I'm frightfully sorry," she said, in much the same tone that she might have used in apologizing to her partner for a double fault at tennis. "But really, Mr. Philipson, I didn't know what to think. It didn't seem——" her voice threatened to waver, but she held it steady, "like you, if you understand. Only, you see," she even laughed, "I've had no experience of murderers."

"No. Of course." Philipson accepted her explanation, but his expression was rather like that of a child who has been snubbed. Justina's camouflage had succeeded, and if she was sorry she had only herself to thank.

"I didn't do it," he said after a considerable silence. "I remembered all about it when I—found old Marshall—in the field. I'd forgotten, you know."

Justina told him that she did know.

"I suppose," Philipson continued, "that it was Yorke?"

Justina realized that he had already been thinking it out. Well, he'd better have it all now, rather than lie worrying about it.

"Yes," she said.

"Did he get away?"

"No."

"Is he in prison?"

"Yes."

Mr. Philipson said nothing for quite a long time. She could see that the thought of Yorke in prison troubled him, but she judged that he could stand it now. At last he said, with a sort of sigh: "He will hate it," and then, after hardly a pause: "He meant to do me in, you know."

Justina thought that she did know. But she also thought that he needed to talk about it.

She said: "Did he?" sympathetically.

"I'd no idea of course," Philipson rambled on. After days of such terrified concealment it was indeed a relief to be able to talk, to anybody, about anything. Besides there were things in his mind which needed an antiseptic, and to talk of them might provide it.

"When I came back from Oldners Farm last night—Not last night? A week ago? Really?" He paused to adjust his ideas: "Well when I got back to Miller's Green, I heard Yorke's car. In fact I saw him come down the lane and turn in. So I went straight to the garage. I was feeling quite idiotic you know, as if I'd been a bit drunk, and the headlights simply blinded me. So I suppose I stood there just grinning and blinking at him, and holding out his pistol in my hand. He was in the car, but he got out."

He stopped. Justina began to wonder if she ought to have let him talk. But she could not stop him now.

"I said something silly like: 'I say, Yorke.' I meant to tell him about finding old Marshall. I never thought——" He pulled himself up and went on again. "He just stuck his head back into the car and switched off the engine and switched out the lights."

He stopped, remembering how the hum of the engine had changed from a low throb to an angry growl, and ceased in a sudden quiet, and how the lights had gone out, and in the darkness and silence Yorke had seemed, quite inexplicably, to have switched himself out of existence together with the light and power of the car.

"It—it was horrid," he said. "Though I suppose I wasn't frightened at the time."

"You've got nothing to be frightened of now," Justina told him firmly, and he agreed, but with rather a doubtful "no."

"Well then I told him: 'It's all right. It's me.' And he said: 'Where are you? I can't see you.'"

"So I said: 'I'm here.' But he only asked again: 'Where are you?' I knew he was coming towards me, and I went on feeling for him. And he caught my hand, the one with the pistol in it, and got behind me somehow, and grabbed my other arm, and I said: 'Look out, you ass,' and the pistol went off." He finished the story in a very small voice.

Justina got up.

"It's time for your medicine," she said cheerfully, and gave it to him. She hoped that now he had got this off his chest he would feel better. But he had not finished.

"I suppose," he went on obstinately, after she had sat down again and taken up her sewing: "I suppose I was badly in his way. All the time he must have been waiting for an opportunity to get rid of old Marshall's body. And I stopped him. Twice—— Yes. One night I dished the car, and the next night he was just starting, and I stopped him going out, and then Tucker came, and then the snow. And then, of course, he couldn't go near the thing.

"I suppose that was why," Philipson was now talking more than half to himself, "that was why he was so mad with me. I suppose—yes, of course, he *wanted* me to commit suicide." He remembered Justina's presence, and threw in a word of explanation. "You see he must have guessed that I saw—it—at Oldners Farm, and that I might remember. But—— I say ——!" He stopped abruptly, and for a long time lay quiet. Justina began again to wonder if she ought not to have put him off somehow. She did not quite like the look of him. He was flushed and frowning.

"Miss Tellwright," he began again suddenly, "does any sleeping draught smell of almonds?"

"Almonds? A sleeping draught?" she said, and could not keep her voice professional and calm. "No."

"Does any poison?"

"Cyanide does," she told him.

"Cyanide," he repeated, and she saw his eyelids flicker as if at the threat of a blow. After a moment, he remarked, in a voice that was rather too casual:

"I must have had a pretty narrow squeak. I sneezed, and the thing tipped off the edge of the table."

His eyes, from wandering round the room, came back to

Justina. He was not an observant man, but even he could not fail to notice how her face had whitened. He stared at her. She looked up and caught his eyes.

"Would you have minded?" he blurted out.

Last week Justina had feared that he was a murderer. Since Sunday she had known that he was not, but instead must fear, first for his life, then for his reason. Now she had learnt that all the time she had suspected him of crime, he had been living, eating, working, alongside a murderer who had determined on his death. It was too much.

Like a child in a tantrum she jumped up from her chair, and threw her sewing on the ground.

"Of course I should!" she answered in a weak but angry shout, and turned her back on him. He must not see that she was crying; it would be a calamity, unendurable, irreparable, if he saw that she was crying; but she could not find her handkerchief.

"Don't!" Mr. Philipson was thumping with his fist upon the bed. "Don't! Oh damn! Stop it, I tell you. Oh! Come *here*, you little silly."

Justina came.

CPSIA information can be obtained
at www.ICGtesting.com
Printed in the USA
BVHW050006140223
658390BV00008B/255